D0747025

CANADA IN HAITI
WAGING WAR ON THE POOR MAJORITY

Yves Engler

Anthony Fenton

RED PUBLISHING

FERNWOOD PUBLISHING

PHOTOS Haiti Information Project, Sasha B. Kramer
COVER DESIGN Working Design   EDITOR Bianca Mugyenyi
Printed and bound in Canada by Transcontinental Printing

A CO-PUBLICATION OF
RED Publishing
2736 Cambridge Street
Vancouver, B.C. V5K 1L7 and
Fernwood Publishing
Site 2A, Box 5, 32 Oceanvista Lane
Black Point, Nova Scotia B0J 1B0
and 324 Clare Avenue
Winnipeg, Manitoba R3L 1S3
www.fernwoodbooks.ca

Fernwood Publishing Company Limited gratefully acknowledges the
financial support of the Department of Canadian Heritage, the Nova
Scotia Department of Tourism and Culture and the Canada Council for
the Arts for our publishing program.

Library and Archives Canada Cataloguing in Publication
Fenton, Anthony
Canada in Haiti / Anthony Fenton, Yves Engler.
Includes index.
ISBN 1-55266-168-7
1. Canada—Foreign relations—Haiti. 2. Haiti—Foreign
relations—Canada. 3. Haiti—Politics and government—1986-.
I. Engler, Yves, 1979- II. Title.
FC251.H34F46 2005 327.7107294'09'051 C2005-904574-4

TABLE OF CONTENTS

GLOSSARY OF ACRONYMS

ADF America's Development Foundation (U.S. "Democracy Enhancing" organization)

ARD, Inc. Associates in Rural Development (U.S. "Democracy Enhancing" organization)

CAII Creative Associates International Incorporated (U.S. "Democracy Enhancing" organization)

CARICOM Caribbean Community

CEPPS Consortium for Elections and Political Process Strengthening (U.S. funded agencies working together)

CIDA Canadian International Development Agency

CHAN Canada Haiti Action Network (Solidarity network)

CIPE Center for International Private Enterprise (One of "four pillar" organizations under NED)

CIVPOL United Nations Civilian Police

DC Democratic Convergence (An umbrella group opposed to Lavalas government)

DFA (Canadian) Department of Foreign Affairs

FADH Former Haitian Armed Forces

FOCAL Foundation for the Americas (Government funded, key strategists for Canadian policy in Haiti)

FRAPH Front for Advancement and Progress (CIA-spawned paramilitary death squads)

G-184 Group of 184 (Umbrella group of political oppo-

sition and business elite founded in December 2002 with
links to Washington-based Haiti Democracy Project)

HAC Haiti Action Committee (San Francisco Bay Area
based solidarity network)

HDP Haiti Democracy Project (U.S. Brookings Institute,
and elite anti-Aristide Haitian backed pressure group)

HNP Haitian National Police

ICHRDD Rights and Democracy (CIDA-funded human
rights NGO with links to the NED)

IFES International Foundation for Election Systems
(Funded by U.S. government)

IRI International Republican Institute (One of "four pillar" organizations under NED)

ISC Civil Society Initiative (Predecessor of G-184, com-
prised mainly of business elite)

MINUSTAH UN Mission in Haiti

NCHR National Coalition for Haitian Rights

NDI National Democratic Institute (Funded by U.S. government, one of "four pillars" under NED)

NED National Endowment for Democracy (Product of
the Reagan era; funded by U.S. government)

NGO Non-governmental organization

SCFAIT (Canadian) Standing Committee on Foreign
Affairs and International Trade

USAID U.S. Agency for International Development

HAITI TIMELINE

Taino and Arawak inhabit Ayiti (mountainous land)
1492 Christopher Columbus claims Hispaniola for Spain
1520s The Spanish first import African slaves
1629 French establish a base in western Hispaniola
1700s French implement system with 128 racial types
1791-1803 Slaves end slavery and defeat European forces
1804 Haiti declares independence from France
1806 Mullatto elite murder independence leader, Jean Jacques Dessallines
1825 Haiti begins payment of 150 million francs to France as reparations, to reimburse slave owners for loss of property
1860-1915 U.S. and European powers repeatedly send gunboats to reclaim odious debt
1915 U.S. creates modern Haitian army
1918 U.S. changes Haitian constitution to allow foreign land ownership
1915-34 United States occupies Haiti
1957 François "Papa Doc" Duvalier becomes president with the support of Haitian army
1964 Papa Doc Duvalier declares himself president-for-life
1971 Jean-Claude "Baby Doc" Duvalier, replaces dead father with backing of U.S. government
1986 Widespread protests force Baby Doc into exile

1990, December 16 Jean-Bertrand Aristide is elected with 67% majority in first free presidential election

1991, September 30 Army coup d'état ousts Aristide

1994, September 19 Multinational forces led by U.S. troops return Aristide, but rather than serve five years to which he was elected, U.S. insists his term end in early 1996

1995, December 17 René Préval elected president

1996 Fanmi Lavalas, led by Aristide, is formed and becomes most popular political party

2000, May 21, July 9 Two rounds of elections and Fanmi Lavalas wins overwhelmingly

2000, November 26 Aristide elected president in election boycotted by many opposition parties

2001, February 7 Aristide sworn in as the opposition Democratic Convergence (DC) creates a parallel government

2001, December 17 National Palace attacked in coup attempt — DC claims government attacked itself

2002, September 4 OAS adopts resolution 822, effectively giving opposition parties veto over resumption of foreign aid

2004, February Former Haitian soldiers invade from Dominican Republic, overrun towns and kill police

2004, February 29 U.S. troops fly Aristide to the Central African Republic as airport is patrolled by Canadian troops

2004, March Gérard Latortue, a resident of Florida for 15 years, is appointed interim prime minister

PREFACE / Democratic Accountability

THE STORY OF HAITI is one of resistance, of a spirit that exists inside us all, to assert our essential humanity. Unfortunately the story is also one of how the rich and powerful feel threatened by this spirit and the lengths they are prepared to go to crush it. The people of Haiti have long endured exploitation by powerful interests who claim to know "what is best" for them. Whether their exploiters have been white French plantation owners, American corporations or a mulatto elite, the descendents of Africans shipped across the Atlantic in one of the greatest genocides the world has ever known, have always fought back. In this they followed the example of the Tainos and Arawaks, the original inhabitants of the Caribbean island, who battled to the last person against European imperialists who stole their land and natural resources while trying to enslave them. Haiti's reality is the result of grim extremes of human misery, oppression and exploitation, but in equal measure, it remains a powerful symbol of hope, born in the only successful large-scale slave rebellion in history.

This book is about the relationship between the country that ranks highest in the Americas on the United

Nations' Human Development Index, Canada, and the hemisphere's lowest ranking nation, Haiti. According to a survey released in June 2005, by the U.S.-based Pew Research Center Global Attitudes Project, 94 percent of Canadians believe their country is well liked around the world, the highest percentage of 16 nations surveyed. Citizens of the "Great White North" believe Canada is a force for good in the world.

Is this perception accurate?

The governments of Canada, France and the USA claim to support democracy around the world. The administration of President George W. Bush even maintains a willingness to wage war in the name of democracy. The UN is supposed to uphold the rule of law and constitutional order. But, since the toppling of Haiti's democratically elected government, a human rights disaster has unfolded. To understand the origin of this disaster is to learn about a side of "international relations" that our governments would prefer to keep hidden.

This book is offered in the spirit of democratic accountability. We strive to tell the truth about what has been done by Canadians (and others) in Haiti. We hope our fellow citizens will feel as we have felt while researching this story and getting to know members of the Haitian community: We are angry that our tax dollars have been spent to overthrow a fledgling democracy and to promote an illegal government that engages in massive human rights violations; We demand the Canadian government be a force for good in Haiti by leaving Haitians to shape their own political, social and economic realities; We are unafraid to state that we write this book in true solidarity with the 'poor majority' of Haitians, those who, as the facts show, have had democracy stolen from them by the very governments who claim to be the bastions of freedom.

1 / The First Nation of Free People in the Americas

"What interests me is the future of Haiti, it is the future of Haitians, it is the progress of democracy, and the progress of the rule of law."
— Foreign Affairs Minister Pierre Pettigrew, June 17, 2005

"From the outset I clearly signaled my intention to have Canada take a leadership role in providing the international support needed to produce a blueprint for Haitian society. ... Democracy is the right of every Haitian citizen. It is a condition absolutely essential to improving the economic and social welfare of each citizen."
— Prime Minister Paul Martin, December 11, 2004

WHILE THE DISPARITY BETWEEN the hemisphere's wealthiest and poorest countries is massive, the gap in the story told by politicians and the North American media about Haiti and what ordinary people in that country believe, is similarly wide. Our introduction to this gap was Jeremy, fun, full of youthful enthusiasm, creativity and passion. He was a 19-year-old photographer from the Delmas neighborhood of Port-au-Prince when Haiti celebrated its 200th birthday on January 1, 2004.

"It should have been a time to celebrate our history," Jeremy said. But rather than enjoy a festive occasion and a nationwide celebration, the Caribbean state of eight million was in turmoil. A destabilization campaign was waged by foreign powers upset by a government that strove to put the needs of poor Haitians before the interests of foreign corporations, the International Monetary Fund and a wealthy elite.

According to Jeremy's version of events, U.S. and Canadian soldiers ousted the democratically elected Haitian government of Jean-Bertrand Aristide on February 29, 2004. A few weeks later, a "council of wise people" picked by the U.S., appointed an interim "illegal" government headed by Gérard Latortue, a man from Florida who had not lived in Haiti for 15 years.

"Haiti was the first nation of free people in the Americas," said Jeremy. The only successful slave rebellion in human history established a state 60 years before the USA's emancipation proclamation. (It wasn't until after this proclamation ending slavery that the U.S. managed to recognize Haiti's independence.) He spoke of how, in August 1791, slaves rose up in the north of France's wealthiest colony (for the slave owners, not the slaves) and their rebellion quickly spread. Soon the brilliant Toussaint L'Ouverture took the lead. "Brothers and friends, I am Toussaint L'Ouverture, my name is perhaps known to you. I have undertaken vengeance. I want liberty and equality to reign in San Domingo [Haiti and Dominican Republic]," said the slave who would be free. These words, said Jeremy, should be as well known as the American Declaration of Independence or the Declaration of the Rights of Man from the French Revolution of 1789. For reasons of race and empire, they remain obscure to this day.

In 1796, the British Empire sent one of its largest-ever expeditionary forces to crush the rebellion and reinstitute slavery because of worries that the "bad example" might spread throughout its colonies in the Caribbean. Instead, L'Ouverture's military victories turned the island into "the burial ground of Great Britain." Soon after, Napoleon Bonaparte sent 35,000 troops to re-conquer France's former colony and restore slavery. (Washington gave $400,000 — a vast sum at the time — to the French effort.) Despite a campaign of terror waged against the Haitian people, Napoleon too was defeated. Spain made similar attempts, sending thousands of troops between 1791 and 1804. Victorious over the military forces of three empires, the freed slaves of Haiti declared independence in 1804. But Toussaint L'Ouverture did not live to see the new country. In a prelude to the centuries of lies and duplicity to come, he was lured to "peace negotiations" but was instead transported across the Atlantic where he died in captivity. Three years after independence the country's first leader, Jean Jacques Dessalines, was murdered by the "lighter skinned" Creole elite in the first of more than 30 coups. As they say in Haiti, "A constitution is paper, the bayonet is steel."

In 1804, as in 2004, Haiti was, to the colonial powers, a "threat of a good example," a poor country that broke from the path of exploitation and chose to chart its own course.

"THE COUP D'ÉTAT OF 1991 showed how terribly afraid the one percent is of the mobilization of the poor. They are afraid of those under the table — afraid they will see what is on the table. Afraid of those in Cité Soleil, that they will become impatient with their own misery. Afraid of the peasants, that they will not be 'moun andeyo' [outsiders] anymore. They are afraid that those who cannot read will learn how to read. They are afraid that those who speak Creole will learn French, and no longer feel inferior. They are afraid of the poor entering the palace, of the street children swimming in the pool. They are not afraid of me. They are afraid that what I say may help the poor to see."
– Jean-Bertrand Aristide *Eyes of the Heart*, 2000

THE GOVERNMENT OF PRESIDENT Jean-Bertrand Aristide was not perfect, said Jeremy, but it offered hope to the millions of desperately poor Haitians who had seldom experienced anything close to democracy. Aristide, a former priest, helped build a movement of ordinary people to challenge the power of the foreign-dominated elite, which reached appalling levels of brutality and exploitation during the 30-year reign of "Papa Doc" and "Baby Doc" Duvalier. Baby Doc was exiled in 1986 by popular unrest. In 1990, Aristide, with 67 percent of the vote, defeated the U.S.-backed candidate, former World Bank official Marc Bazin.

But Aristide's first government lasted only seven months until it was overthrown in September 1991 by a CIA-backed military coup. A worldwide outcry and a wave of "boat people" fleeing Haiti, together with the brutality and drug dealing of the illegal government, compelled the Clinton administration to send 20,000 troops to the island in 1994, returning Aristide to the presidency. He governed until 1996, when Haiti saw its first democratic transfer of power after René Préval, an associate of Aristide, won handily in the 1995 elections.

In May 2000, Aristide's Fanmi Lavalas party won an overwhelming victory in elections for about 7,500 local and nation-wide positions. A report of the Organization of American States described the elections this way: "The day was a great success for the Haitian population which turned out in large and orderly numbers to choose both their local and national governments and for the Haitian National Police." The report noted some irregularities in the tallying of votes and the failure to count others, but concluded that "since one political party [Fanmi Lavalas] won most of the elections by a substantial margin, it is unlikely that the majority of the final outcomes in local elections have been affected."

In the face of this overwhelming victory and a certain win for Aristide in the November 2000 presidential elections, the response of the Haitian elite and their foreign backers was to declare the elections tainted. They said eight of 27 Senate seats should have gone to runoff elections. But, even without the disputed senators Fanmi Lavalas still had a majority in the senate. Instead of working inside the democratic system to improve the lives of ordinary Haitians, the elite plotted the overthrow of a government it did not control. And for this, they received significant aid from foreign governments. Pressured by the new George W. Bush administration, which seemed to view Aristide and a democratic Haiti with particular contempt, most western governments suspended aid. Instead, money was channeled into "democracy enhancing" groups that worked to undermine the government.

"We are poor and need help," said Jeremy. "But instead wealthy countries spend their money on making life worse for us. Why do they hate us?"

This question hangs over recent events in Haiti like an unspoken family secret.

WITHIN FIVE WEEKS OF HAITI'S 200-year anniversary celebrations, the country was in the grips of an armed insurrection. On February 5, 2004, in Gonaïves, insurgents killed police and took control of the country's fourth largest city. Initially Canadian Foreign Affairs Minister Bill Graham denounced the rebellion, saying that Canada supported Aristide's elected government. On February 12, U.S. Secretary of State, Colin Powell told the Senate foreign relations committee: "The policy of the [Bush] administration is not regime change. President Aristide is the elected president of Haiti." And he reaffirmed that five days later. "We cannot buy into a proposition that says the elected president must be forced out of office by thugs and those who do not respect law and are bringing terrible violence to the Haitian people."

The force of former Haitian soldiers (from an army disbanded by Aristide) swept through the country, beginning with St. Marc, an important port city. Then on February 22, Cap Haïtien, the country's second largest city, fell to the insurgents. Scores of police officers were killed and many more simply abandoned their posts to the better-armed rebels. As the insurgents made their way to Port-au-Prince, the international community, (including Paul Martin's Liberal government) ignored the elected government's requests for "a few dozen" peacekeepers to restore order in a country without an army.

On February 26, three days before Aristide's removal, the OAS permanent council called on the UN Security Council to, "take all the necessary and appropriate urgent measures to address the deteriorating situation in Haiti." The Caribbean Community (CARICOM) called upon the UN Security Council to deploy an emergency military task force to assist Aristide's government. This appeal for assistance was flatly rejected by the world's most powerful nations, exposing their pro-coup position.

By the end of the month, gunmen had overrun all major cities except for Port-au-Prince and rebels set up on the outskirts. Supporters of the elected president built barricades across the capital. They blocked the main arteries of the city of two million and prepared to fight. Even with most of the country in rebel hands, the government's prospects began to improve as pro-government police recaptured several cities. A shipment of guns, bulletproof vests and ammunition was in Kingston, Jamaica, en route from South Africa at the request of CARICOM. Rumors were swirling that Venezuela had agreed to send soldiers to protect the constitutional government. Most important, Port-au-Prince's size makes it difficult for a few hundred men to capture; rebels were likely not capable of seizing the capital while holding on to the cities they had already overrun.

But the battle for Port-au-Prince never took place. In

the early hours of February 29, 2004, U.S. soldiers, with Canadian forces "securing" the airport, escorted Haiti's elected president and his security staff onto a jet and out of the country. A new UN force quickly took charge of the country, along with an interim government appointed by a council of "wise people" put together by France, Canada and the USA. Canadian and U.S. officials insisted the president had resigned to avoid a bloodbath, a version of events accepted by most of the world's media despite Aristide's contradictory account. He claimed to have been forced from office by U.S. troops. One of Aristide's U.S.-based security guards confirmed the president was kidnapped. Referring to the U.S. version of events he said, "That was just bogus. It's a story they fabricated."

Who is more believable? Why would Aristide lie? Only a few days before supposedly "voluntarily" resigning Aristide said he was prepared to die fighting the rebellion. Why did the U.S. take Aristide to the Central African Republic (without telling him or his wife where they were going) when Miami is only an hour away by air from Port-au-Prince? Why did the U.S., France and Canada send troops to Haiti on or before February 28, but not earlier when the elected government asked for them? Why did U.S. Coast Guard vessels get an emergency call to patrol Haiti's waters two weeks before Aristide's ouster? Why was the UN able to pass a motion calling for intervention to stabilize Haiti on

March 1, but not on February 26? Why has UN Secretary General Kofi Annan ignored the demands of CARICOM and the African Union for an investigation into Aristide's removal? Why, since the intervention by Canadian, U.S. and UN-led troops, has the economic, social and human rights situation deteriorated significantly?

"WHAT WE NEED is to move from elections to elections, not coup d'état to coup d'état. ... But there is clearly a small minority in Haiti with their allies in foreign countries. Together, they said no to elections, because they knew once they respect the will of the people in a democratic way through free, fair democratic elections, then they will not be able to continue to live in a country where they don't pay tax, where they still have the wall of apartheid, where they continue to consider the coup as if there were not human beings, and so and so. ... The United States, France, Canada and so many others should do something to repair, if they can, what they did. Because what they did is a crime. The same way slavery is a crime against humanity, the same way what they're doing against the Haitian people, it's also a crime. And all of that we can put it in this process of maintaining a black holocaust in Haiti."

Aristide, interviewed by Amy Goodman from exile in South Africa, May 2005

A FEW MONTHS AFTER Aristide was ousted, Jeremy was in exile and his aunt was dead — killed by armed thugs who were searching for him. An aspiring young journalist with the state television network, Jeremy was one of thousands of Haitians hunted down for their affiliation with the elected government. "In your country, is it a crime to want a better life?" he asked. He returned to Port-au-Prince in December 2004. "Here, the rich and powerful seem to want democracy made illegal."

2 / Responsibility to Protect or A Made-in-Ottawa Coup?

MANY OF THOSE WHO DEFEND Aristide's removal and the subsequent events cite a doctrine that argues powerful countries must "protect" weak countries whenever perceived necessary. The Canadian government, beginning under Jean Chrétien, has taken the lead on a UN reform initiative called the "Responsibility to Protect," which would effectively rewrite international law to allow military intervention in certain cases as a means of assisting "failing and failed states." But what and who defines a "failed" state? Are the factors leading to the "failure" of a state relevant? If a country has been subject to destabilizing factors (such as economic embargo, foreign funding of political opposition groups, training and arming of paramilitaries), should this be taken into account when deciding what the international community ought to do about the "failed" state? If there is to be an international law that allows foreign intervention in certain cases, should there not also be a law that prohibits destabilization campaigns by rich and powerful countries? If not, the "Responsibility to Protect" may just be another name for colonialism.

Powerful countries have made a habit of interfering in

the affairs of weaker states and such practices are certainly not new to Haiti. Indeed, the U.S. narrative concerning Haitian independence in the 1800s regarded the "Negro empire" as doomed to "failure." History has demonstrated that the U.S. and other Western powers did their utmost to guarantee Haiti's perpetual "failure."

Guatemala, Congo, Iran, Dominican Republic, Chile, Grenada and Nicaragua are a small sample of other countries whose governments were "destabilized" out of existence over the past half century. Historians later wrote about the causes and effects. Rather than simply describe events of long ago, our goal is more substantive. We hope to influence the current state of affairs. We believe Haitians can overcome the injustice inflicted upon them. The first step is to educate people of good intentions about how forces of greed and deceit got their way.

The destabilization of Haiti was multifaceted. It included "civil society building," military and paramilitary interventions, an economic embargo that would cripple the hemisphere's poorest nation, a full-scale disinformation campaign waged by Haitian elite-owned and international corporate media, and concerted diplomatic efforts directed at guaranteeing regime change would be both acceptable to the international community and believable to a confused public.

We ask the reader's patience with a complex story. (To help make sense of the various groups named, there is a glossary of acronyms on pages 4 and 5.) Many details of the destabilization campaign will remain unknown until documents are declassified. That said, enough is on the public record to tell the following:

WE BEGIN IN 1994, with Aristide's return to power by U.S. marines. This was hailed as a great democratic deed, yet the scent of previous destabilization lingered. Despite being the overwhelming electoral choice of Haitians, some important individuals did not trust Aristide or his Lavalas movement. This resulted in the strengthening of various barriers and limitations to sovereignty. The most obvious barrier was the U.S. refusal to disband and bring to justice the death squads they helped create during 1991-94. FRAPH, a CIA-trained and funded paramilitary was not properly disarmed after the U.S. invasion and subsequent UN occupation. The elected government lacked the resources to demilitarize Haitian society on its own and so perpetrators of serious crimes went unpunished. The U.S. also confiscated 160,000 documents detailing activities of FRAPH and the military regime, confounding efforts to bring justice and closure to the Haitian people who endured its death squads for three years. As Jane Regan wrote in Covert Action Quarterly in 1995, "Rather than disarm the Haitian army and its para-military assistants as promised in writing to the Aristide government, or purge the human rights violators, the U.S.

is now in effect overseeing a kind of massive School of the Americas for the entire Haitian armed forces." Regan noted that Aristide's government was spending too many resources battling the infiltration of Haiti's security forces to adequately deal with "fighting U.S. development schemes and democracy enhancement projects."

Regan accurately summarized the difficulties that Haiti's democracy confronted: "Behind closed doors, U.S. Agency for International Development (AID), the World Bank, the National Endowment for Democracy (NED), and scores of U.S.-funded groups are institutionalizing a more permanent, less reversible invasion. The troops of this intervention, called democracy enhancement by AID and low intensity democracy by others, are technicians and experts. Their weapons are development projects and lots of money. Their goal is to impose a neoliberal economic agenda, to undermine grassroots democracy, to create political stability conducive to a good business climate, and to bring Haiti into the new world order append-aged to the U.S. as a source for markets and cheap labor." (Neoliberalism is commonly known as liberalized trade and investment, privatizations and fiscal austerity.)

Rather than acting out of a "responsibility to protect" Haiti, powerful U.S. interests helped themselves. In a Z Magazine article outlining various aspects of the economic policy forced upon a returned Aristide and the Haitian people — including the reduction of tariffs to allow the dumping of U.S. chicken parts and rice — Noam Chomsky stated the obvious; social breakdown would be the inevitable outcome.

All through the mid 1990s the International Republican Institute (IRI) funded opposition groups in the name of "democracy enhancement" — buzzwords justifying foreign involvement in Haiti's political affairs — in a fashion that would be illegal in IRI's homeland. (Laws prohibit foreign funding of U.S. political parties.) IRI was a crucial component in the destabilization of Haiti. An organization acting on behalf of U.S. foreign policy worldwide, the IRI is one of the "four pillar" organizations operating under the National Endowment for Democracy (NED). In *Killing Hope: U.S. Military and CIA Interventions Since WWII,* William Blum cites Allen Weinstein, the man who helped create the legislation that gave rise to the NED in the 1980s under Reagan: "A lot of what we [NED] do today was done covertly 25 years ago by the CIA." When this book went to print, Weinstein worked as an advisor for IFES, a sister organization of NED and IRI that also played a significant role in Haiti's coup.

According to Eva Golinger, author of *The Chavez Code,* the IRI is run, "by a Board of Directors that reads like a right-wing parade." In Haiti, the IRI aided right-leaning political parties with lessons on how to mobilize and capture media attention as well as conducting numerous

surveys on political opinions and attitudes. IRI also played
host to conferences aimed at consolidating the opposition. During the 1995 elections the IRI complained bit-
terly, threatening to cut off U.S. government aid after the
defeat of the candidates they had supported. To shed light
upon the sort of people associated with the group, one
need only look at who led the 1995 election observation
delegation sent by IRI to Haiti: Porter Goss, a former CIA
agent turned Republican congressman who would later be
appointed director of the CIA.

This foreign meddling upset many Haitians. A 1998
Associated Press article explained: "The international arm
of the U.S. Republican Party [IRI] is embroiled in a political
storm in Haiti, where its crusade for political pluralism is
being condemned as support for militarist right-wing parties ... The Haitian News Network said IRI was engaged in
'overthrowing the Haitian political order,' and that 'certain
pieces of information lead one to believe that a certain sector of the U.S. establishment supports [a destabilization]
movement through IRI.'"

To deflect the criticism, those orchestrating the destabilization campaign put the best possible spin on their activities. A 1998 quarterly report of IRI's activities in Haiti stated the IRI's "Democracy Support Program" was designed
to address "critical deficiencies in Haiti's democratic culture and political system." IRI played host to a series of

"political dialogue forums" that effectively gave support to figures such as former president Leslie Manigat, key opposition leader Evans Paul and former U.S.-backed presidential candidate Marc Bazin. These politicians would all play central roles in the phase of destabilization that regained momentum in 2000. Stating "IRI remains at the center of a debate on democracy in Haiti," the report described how newspapers such as Haiti-Progrès denounced their activities and the resistance they encountered to their programs. Eventually, the IRI was forced to shut down their Haiti office, retreating to the Dominican Republic.

Despite the pressure, U.S.-backed "democracy enhancement" shifted into higher gear because the Haitian constitution permitted Aristide to run for president again in 2000. In February 1999, UN Secretary General Kofi Annan warned that Haiti would be cut off from international assistance unless the country's leaders began to "pursue constructive and meaningful negotiations to resolve the crisis." In July, UN Wire news service reported that, "Haiti will not receive $570 million in aid from the World Bank and the Inter-American Development Bank this year because of the two-year political stalemate in the country."

What was the crisis? One can only speculate. The panic may have been produced by IRI's forced departure in 1998, the end to U.S. police training and the refusal to privatize all state owned companies. The 1997 legislative elections in Haiti under President Préval saw Aristide's new Fanmi Lavalas Party (which had split from the Lavalas Political Organization — OPL) make significant gains in the senate. The opposition seized upon a low voter turnout to question the vote's legitimacy. But, according to AP reporter Michael Norton on April 8, 1997: "Many Haitians who boycotted the vote were bitter that legislators in October had approved an economic program that has raised food prices and eliminated many jobs." Another central election issue was the neoliberal plan of the U.S. and other international donors. AP: "At stake is an internationally driven economic program tied to tens of million of dollars in foreign aid. Aristide's party wants to challenge the program and could win the seats it needs to do so through the elections. Representatives of donor governments and international monetary institutions fear it could slow down or block the plan to modernize the economy." The real fear was that Haitians preferred to do what was good for their country, not what was good for the World Bank. While the Clinton administration praised the 1997 elections as free and fair, Republican observers condemned the elections, calling for more intense "civic education" programs. This "crisis" would endure until 1999, when the international embargo began in earnest.

BEFORE HAITI'S MAY 2000 parliamentary elections, the U.S. gave considerable support to non-Lavalas political parties and candidates. At least $410,000 was devoted to "the provision of funds for the purchase of media air time to promote the parties' candidates for parliamentary seats, and their platforms." While the support was premised on "bipartisanship" an Associates in Rural Development, Inc (ARD, Inc) report showed that opposition parties would be most likely to take advantage of it. Other reports indicated that the political opposition was not nearly organized enough to pose a serious challenge to Fanmi Lavalas. The post-election OAS-led denunciation of the vote tallying process (see below) was therefore very convenient for the opposition. Indeed, even before the ballots had been cast, leader of a fringe party (and former president), Leslie Manigat declared, "We really need to form a front. We need to form ... the democratic convergence to speak with one voice, to put pressure, to be watchful and to prevent fraud from distorting the results." The Democratic Convergence made its official debut in July 2000, calling for President Préval to step down and for the May elections to be annulled. The DC also announced plans to boycott the November presidential elections. Again, the emergence of the DC and its boycott policy were a convenient excuse for Washington to turn the screws on Aristide a little tighter.

In September 2000, U.S. Secretary of State Madeleine Albright convened a meeting of "the friends of Haiti." Foreign Affairs Minister Lloyd Axworthy was Canada's representative. The meeting resulted in a U.S. declaration that they would withdraw assistance for Haiti's November presidential elections. Was it yet another coincidence that Gallup polls predicted a landslide victory for Aristide? Results of a USAID poll of 1,002 Haitians conducted nationwide by CID-Gallup in October, 2000, showed 92.8 percent of those surveyed knew about the upcoming presidential elections and the vast majority said they were very likely (55.9 percent) or somewhat likely (22.7 percent) to vote. Nearly 65 percent believed there were no major obstacles holding of national elections. Over 50 percent chose Aristide as the most trusted national leader in Haiti and no member of the opposition came anywhere near that figure. Fanmi Lavalas was the preferred party by 13 to one. That Aristide was expected to win was no secret to anyone. Like the playground bully who can't get his way, the opposition DC wouldn't play if it couldn't win.

Despite the opposition's inability to win at the ballot box, DC gained strength by deliberating independently with the OAS. In October, Agence France Presse reported "Despite efforts by the Organization of American States to smooth things over, no agreement could be reached [concerning the boycott] between Aristide's party, the Lavalas Family Party, and the opposition, organized under the Democratic Convergence Party." OAS representative Luigi Einuadi would emerge as the "go-to" person to "resolve the impasse." Was he an impartial observer? Einuadi was a longtime defender of the School of the Americas where the U.S. military trained Latin American officers, many of whom went on to terrorize their populations. On the eve of Haiti's bicentennial, December 31, 2003, Einuadi told a small group of people "The real problem in Haiti is that the international community is so screwed up and divided that they are letting Haitians run Haiti."

The propaganda effort to discredit the elections and, by extension, Fanmi Lavalas, began with the OAS reversal of their earlier election assessment on the basis of a technicality, claiming that the counting method used for eight Senate seats was "flawed". The Haitian constitution stipulates that the winner must get 50 percent plus one vote at the polls; the CEP (Coalition d'Election Provisional) determined this by calculating the percentages from the votes for the top four candidates, while the OAS contended that the count should include all candidates. OAS concerns about the validity of the elections were disingenuous — they worked with the CEP to prepare the elections since 1999 and were fully aware of the counting method beforehand. The same procedure was used in prior elections, but they failed to voice any concerns until Lavalas' landslide victory. Finally, using the OAS method would not have altered the outcome of the elections.

The economic and diplomatic arenas were not the only

active areas of the destabilization campaign. Just days after the OAS announcement, news emerged of "coup and assassination plotting" by seven Haitian police officers, among them Guy Philippe and Jean-Jacques "Jackie" Nau. (Nau is the son-in-law of Foreign Affairs Minister Herard Abraham and served as his chief of security at press time. Philippe was trained by the U.S. in Ecuador.) All seven were arrested during their flight from Haiti into the Dominican Republic. On Oct. 19, 2000, AP quoted secretary of Dominican armed forces Miguel Soto saying that, "It seems they [Philippe and Nau] were implicated in a coup d'état." Immediately after the coup plans were exposed, one of Haiti's opposition leaders, Gerard Pierre Charles (OPL Party), blamed the "supposed conspiracy" on Aristide and Préval, whom, he baselessly charged with attempting "to derail talks brokered by the OAS to end the opposition boycott and allow a competitive presidential election."

Word of U.S. involvement in the coup attempt surfaced as the Spanish Efe News Agency noted reports of "an alleged meeting between the policemen accused of promoting a plot to overthrow the government and a U.S. embassy official ..." A February 2, 2001, Washington Post article would confirm that Donald Steinberg, an aide to the U.S. ambassador at the time, relayed intelligence to Haitian authorities concerning the coup plot and possible assassination attempts. Philippe and the others were granted asylum by Dominican authorities, but it would not be long before they were heard from again.

The political opposition's boycott of the November 2000 presidential election proceeded with the opposition becoming increasingly intransigent. Using the "big lie" technique popularly identified with George Orwell's novel *1984*, they claimed public support for their boycott was proven by low voter turnout. On the contrary, Haitian officials and some 3,000 independent observers reported that over four million voters (more than half the total population) registered, 60 percent of whom voted. These figures were better than the 2000 U.S. election and Aristide's 92 percent vote was proportionally almost double what George W. Bush received.

Given Aristide's overwhelming victory, the "international community" had no choice but to recognize him as legitimately elected. But at Aristide's first international event, the 2001 Summit of the Americas in Québec City, Prime Minister Jean Chrétien reportedly "lectured" Aristide on the "shortcomings" of the May elections. Chrétien and other leaders would focus on the need to negotiate with the opposition and called for greater OAS intervention. The international community largely put the onus on Aristide to resolve the problems resulting from the May 2000 elections.

On July 28, 2001, there were several attacks on police stations. Haitian government officials called this a "new attempt at a putsch, which aims at overthrowing President Jean-Bertrand Aristide." DC leaders shifted blame for the attacks once more, claiming, "This certainly looks like a staged event, a preliminary step in a repressive campaign against the opposition."

As DC leaders announced plans to set up a parallel government to protest the incoming Aristide government in January 2001, the U.S. embassy applauded coinciding efforts made by "civil society and business leaders ... to propose solutions to the crisis." Around the same time, high-profile members of the DC, including Leslie Manigat, were invited to attend George W. Bush's inauguration ceremony in Washington. Within weeks of Aristide taking office the Civil Society Initiative (ISC) emerged, announcing their intention to mediate the political crisis. One of the leaders of the ISC, Rosny Desroches, was a neo-Duvalierist who supported the first coup against Aristide. One indication of Desroches' connection to U.S. agencies was the $500,000 his organization, FONHEP, a private education foundation, received from USAID in 1999-2000. Another member of the ISC, the Center for Free Enterprise and Democracy (CLED), received $707,895 in 1999. CLED was also a longtime recipient of funding from the Center for International Private Enterprise (CIPE), one of the "four pillar" organizations operating under the NED.

With George W. Bush's inauguration in 2001, Aristide's days were numbered. As FOCAL's Carlo Dade explained after the 2004 coup, "The Aristide regime was doomed with the 2000 elections in the United States. The United States government had an active policy of supporting the opposition in undermining Aristide."

How active was this policy? Did it include backing paramilitaries? We know that Guy Philippe was implicated in yet another coup attempt, in December 2001. This one was perhaps the most serious, as a reported 39 gunmen stormed the national palace killing four people and briefly occupying the building. One of the captured attackers (five were killed by police) fingered Philippe as a mastermind. A January 2, 2002, Latin American Weekly report described the testimony of captured gunman and former army sergeant Pierre Richardson: "Richardson claimed to have been present at a meeting in Santo Domingo where the raid was planned, under the direction of former police chiefs Guy Philippe and Jean-Jacques Nau."

But, once again, violence against Lavalas was turned inside out by opposition leaders. One of these leaders, Gerard Gourge, stated, "I don't know what happened at the national palace, but it has become a pretext to massacre the opposition." Other articles would build on this spin, pointing out how "Mr. Aristide's machete-wielding supporters [poured] onto the streets in vengeful protest."

Reports circulated about how DC headquarters and offices were torched by angry Aristide supporters in response to the coup attempt.

Two months earlier, in October 2001, President Bush appointed neoconservative Roger Noriega as U.S. ambassador to the OAS. He worked closely with Einuadi and Canadian OAS ambassador David Lee on a unique solution to the crisis fueled by Noriega's U.S. agency counterparts. During confirmation hearings for assistant secretary of state for the western hemisphere two years later, Noriega (who also played a role in the Iran-Contra scandal and worked closely with racist anti-Aristide senator Jesse Helms) revealed that he co-authored OAS Resolutions 806 and 822. These resolutions required the elected government to make decisions together with the opposition, giving non-elected parties an effective veto over resumption of foreign aid to the Haitian government. All the while money continued to pour into U.S.-backed "civil society" groups.

Largely due to the intransigence of the opposition, the OAS resolutions were not fulfilled. Aristide convinced the seven disputed Fanmi Lavalas (one was from another party) senators to resign so that new elections could be held, however, this satisfied neither the opposition nor Noriega. As Canadian think tank FOCAL pointed out in a June 2001 policy paper, "The political opposition so far has rejected Aristide's overtures and the reconciliation process is unlikely to get off the ground if it cannot be brought on board. In all likelihood, the international community will have to continue to put pressure on both sides for things to move ahead." Several other widely distributed reports blamed the deadlock on the opposition's unwillingness to negotiate. In 2002, CARICOM pleaded with Secretary of State Colin Powell to lift the aid embargo on Aristide's government, stating it had fulfilled all demands. The U.S. was not interested.

While OAS Secretary General Cesar Gaviria condemned the attacks on the national palace, he equally condemned the retaliatory targeting of opposition buildings. After sustained media attention on the retaliation by Lavalas sympathizers, it began to seem as though the coup never happened and that the only crimes were attacks against the opposition. The OAS decreed that the Aristide government should pursue "the prosecution of any person, and dismissal, when appropriate, of any person found to be complicit in the violence of December 17, 2001."

Again, this blatant interference in their country's affairs angered many Haitians. Haiti-Progrès summarized a Council On Hemispheric Affairs report that put OAS involvement into context: "(COHA) pointed out in a typically feisty analysis released Jan. 15: 'Another problem with OAS intervention is that it will weaken the country's democratic fabric and will most likely further alienate the Haitian electorate. Most Haitians are already deeply embittered that the U.S. favors the Convergence coalition, and its ending of direct aid, as well as and by imposing a 'semi-blockade' on the country which further impoverishes its impoverished population.' The report also noted: 'After the Dec. 17 failed coup attempt, many Haitians living in Miami carried signs declaring, 'Aristide is the people's choice — not President Bush.' If the OAS is allowed to intervene in this domestic situation on entirely spurious grounds, it could set a dangerous precedent for other member states.'"

While Haitians directed their anger at the U.S. and OAS, Canada and the European Union decided to hop on board with them. They terminated aid to the Aristide government, instead dealing directly with Haitian NGOs mostly aligned with the minority anti-Aristide movement. USAID- and Canadian International Development Agency (CIDA)-funded organizations infiltrated grassroots organizations while developing propaganda campaigns [aka 'civic education'] for dozens of community radio stations throughout Haiti. Organizations such as the America's Development Foundation (ADF), Creative Associates International, Inc. (and their Canadian counterpart Réseau Liberté), IFES, and ARD, Inc., would devote tens of millions of dollars to the destabilization campaign.

Despite this foreign interference, on April 30, 2002, the

Food and Agriculture Organization presented Aristide with the World Food Day gold Medal, "in recognition of his campaign against hunger in Haiti." The FAO cited the economic conditions Aristide was facing, stating that, "even as the United States holds up more than $500 million in aid to the country, Aristide works with domestic and international groups, both public and private, to secure food for Haitians."

The next step in the destabilization campaign began in November 2002, with the inauguration of the Haiti Democracy Project (HDP), sponsored by the Washington-based neo-conservative Brookings Institution. The list of attendees demonstrated the HDP's powerful connections. It included Roger Noriega, OAS Assistant Secretary Einuadi, long-time Democracy Enhancement Project facilitator Ira Lowenthal, James Morrell, Alice Blanchet, powerful Haitian businessman Rudolph Boulos and former U.S. ambassadors to Haiti Timothy Carney and Ernest H. Preeg.

Next, in December 2002, the ISC, in need of a broader platform, spawned the Group of 184 (the number of Haitian organizations then participating in U.S. backed "democracy enhancement" projects). When the Group of 184 made its public debut, its spokesman was Andy Apaid Jr., owner of several Port-au-Prince factories allegedly engaged in sweatshop practices (for companies like Montréal-based Gildan Activewear). Apaid was later linked to the funding and arming of anti-Lavalas death squads. (Intimately connected to the HDP, Apaid's close associate, Reginald Boulos — head of Haiti's Chamber of Commerce — is the brother of Rudolph Boulos, a member of the HDP board.)

The HDP, while not officially affiliated with the G-184, quickly embraced its "social contract," issued in December 2002. Wrote HDP representatives Ira Lowenthal and Clothilde Charlot in a January 2003 South Florida Sun Sentinel editorial: "The recent joint declaration of 184 Haitian civil society organizations signals that a new day may yet dawn amid Haiti's division and despair, 17 years after the end of the Duvalier dictatorship. Now Haitians once again appear ready to unite in the higher interests of the nation, placing their faith not in one leader but in the democratic process itself ... The declaration is nothing short of revolutionary when seen against the backdrop of Haiti's strife-torn history and current crisis.... *The United States should position itself to provide significant support — technical, financial and diplomatic — to this coalition's efforts to turn the tide in Haiti.* [emphasis added]" Indeed, the U.S. and Canada would provide "significant support" to this coalition.

From January 31 - February 1, 2003, Canada's Secretary of State for Latin America and La Francophonie, Denis Paradis, played host to a high-level roundtable meeting dubbed "The Ottawa Initiative on Haiti." In a manner that would foreshadow future meetings hosted by

the Canadian government, no representatives of Haiti's
elected government were invited. Indeed, the Ottawa
Initiative now appears as a dry run at the trusteeship
that was to come. Otto Reich, then Bush's controversial
appointee as Assistant Secretary of State for the Western
Hemisphere, attended the Ottawa meetings. OAS representative Einuadi was there as well.

Paradis leaked news of the Ottawa meeting to his friend
and reporter Michel Vastel. In the March 15, 2003 edition
of L'Actualité magazine, Vastel wrote that the possibility
of Aristide's departure, the need for a potential trusteeship over Haiti, and the return of Haiti's dreaded military
were discussed by Paradis and the French Minister for La
Francophonie, Pierre-André Wiltzer. Paradis would later
deny the report, on the basis that the discussions could
be boiled down to the "Responsibility to Protect."

After details of the Ottawa Initiative were leaked,
key figures in Haiti's opposition condemned the Ottawa
meeting. Evans Paul, former mayor of Port-au-Prince and
ally of Aristide, turned DC opposition leader, denounced
the secret meeting, but welcomed the intervention only a
year later. When this book went to press he was running
for president in elections scheduled for late 2005. Leslie
Manigat, a former president (in the post-Duvalier, pre-
democracy period) wrote a letter (mysteriously included
in declassified government documents obtained by the

authors) that included a statement read on a Miami-based Haitian television show by host Gérard Latortue. A former minister in Manigat's government, Latortue was installed as Prime Minister one year later. It later emerged that Latortue was working closely with IFES, whose chair William Hybl, also sits on the Board of IRI. (Many, if not most members of the "interim government" worked at one time for one of the alphabet soup of groups receiving U.S. government funding.)

Reactions to the Vastel-Paradis leak were actively monitored, as revealed in e-mail obtained through the Access to Information Act. In the correspondence between Canadian Ambassador to Haiti, Kenneth Cook and the Department of Foreign Affairs, Cook pointed out that of the 70 letters received by L'Actualité on the topic of Haitian regime change, "most were positive."

The Liberal government assured the Haitian government that there were no plans for "regime change" and affirmed their commitment to (Noriega's) OAS Resolution 822. Radio Metropole reported on March 19, 2003, that Paradis sent a letter to Haiti's foreign minister telling him that the Ottawa meeting posed no threat to the elected government. But, neither Vastel nor L'Actualité retracted the story. In several post-coup interviews (for example CBC radio, August, 2004 with Haitian-Canadian journalist Jean Saint-Vil and in later interviews with one of the authors) Vastel stood firmly behind his original article, insisting that the French government corroborated Paradis' information. Vastel asserted that several follow-up meetings took place involving the same participants. One of these meetings took place days before the coup with then Secretary of State Colin Powell.

The documents that could clarify this matter — the copy of recommendations made by Paradis and Wiltzer — were blacked out by the DFA in the papers released under our access to information request. (The person with final say on the release of these documents was Christian Lapointe, head of the Latin America and Caribbean desk and primary contact person for the Ottawa Initiative meeting as shown in the very same documents.)

A few months after the Ottawa meeting it became clear that the military option was under active consideration, at least in some quarters. Guy Philippe and four others, including Paul Arcelin, were arrested by Dominican authorities. Arcelin, a Haitian and former professor at the Université du Québec à Montréal, later proclaimed himself "intellectual author" and "political leader" of the military uprising that ousted Aristide. Quoted in an Associated Press story May 7, 2003, a Dominican military official said: "These people are being investigated because of allegations that they are trying to reach Haiti with the aim of conspiring" against the democratically elected government. Arcelin's relationship with Philippe (see next chapter) revealed the connection between the paramilitaries and the U.S.-backed DC opposition, whose representative in the Dominican was Arcelin.

The final consolidation of the opposition took place in late 2003, with the creation of the Democratic Platform (DP). The mandate of the DP, which brought together the G-184 and DC, was the unconditional removal of Aristide from office. In early December, the G-184 sent a letter to the OAS calling on it to "reconsider its current strategy regarding the political crisis in Haiti, building on lessons learned and the window of opportunity created by the unification of traditionally divided sectors of Haitian society through the Group of 184."

Posing as representatives of the Haitian masses, the G-184 mobilized against the government. Numerous demonstrations were organized in the months leading up to the coup. A violent protest at the state university spurred on the G-184 efforts to demonize Lavalas. The OAS followed the G-184's lead, condemning "the violent and unjustified actions in Port-au-Prince Friday, December 5, 2003, of certain members of popular organizations associated with Fanmi Lavalas in attacking students, property, and facilities of the Faculté de Sciences Humaines de l'UEH et de l'INAGHEI, institutions of higher learning in this nation. On this occasion, the HNP regrettably failed in its duty to serve and protect persons and property." Film footage of these events released by journalist Kevin Pina in early 2005 would call into question the narrative, but in late 2003 it quickly became accepted reality, fuelling opposition efforts. The university's rector, Pierre Paquiot, who had his legs broken by unknown assailants (labeled Lavalas partisans) was flown out of the country and attended an IFES press conference in Washington to denounce the Aristide government.

In the following weeks the DP mobilized large demonstrations and called for general strikes. This helped create a climate of insecurity and tension that would cast the final paramilitary incursion in a more justifiable light. In early February 2004, Haiti's "rebels," led by many of the same figures that participated in preceding military efforts, entered the country from the Dominican Republic.

A fair-minded person might ask: Was Haiti a "failed state" or did the world fail to protect the hemisphere's poorest country from the world's most powerful?

3 / Using NGOs to Destroy Democracy and the Canadian Military Connection

IMAGINE A PLAN TO provide Canadians their education, healthcare, water, and welfare through private foreign-government-funded charities, corporations and wealthy individuals. How would most Canadians react to this proposal? How about if these same private charities provided funds to opposition parties and supported the armed takeover of Parliament? Could they be regarded as coherent if they justified these acts in the name of building democracy? It is safe to say most Canadians would view this as an insane plot to return the country to nineteenth-century conditions. Yet, in Haiti, supposedly progressive NGOs from Canada and other countries have promoted just this sort of "democracy building."

The U.S. returned Aristide to office in 1994 with the understanding that he would implement an economic agenda proposed by his defeated opponent from the 1990 election. Aristide was to further downsize the state, or as the World Bank put it: "The renovated state must focus on an economic strategy centered on the energy and initiative of Civil Society, especially the private sector, both national and foreign." International creditors argued that the flipside of this government downsizing would be increased aid, particularly to private sector NGOs. This "aid" money was to be channeled towards projects such as schools and hospitals run by private (usually non-profit) NGOs. This vision fits perfectly with one enunciated earlier, at the time of the creation of the NED, described succinctly by William I. Robinson in *Promoting Polyarchy: Globalization, US Intervention and Hegemony*. He argues that the shift from direct CIA involvement to the NED was a product of a change in U.S. foreign policy from "earlier strategies to contain social and political mobilization through a focus on control of the state and governmental apparatus" to "democracy promotion," in which "the United States and local elites thoroughly penetrate civil society, and from therein, assure control over popular mobilization and mass movements…" In reality, "democracy promotion" can be understood as a means (democratic or otherwise) to benefit the elite of the U.S.A.

Or the elite in Canada.

A CIDA report released in 2005 stated that by 2004, "non-governmental actors (for-profit and not-for-profit) provided almost 80 percent of [Haiti's] basic services." While an NGO-run school may be better than no school at all, a cluster of privately run schools is not an ideal development model. Canada's development agency has admitted as much. According to CIDA, "Supporting non-governmental actors contributed to the creation of parallel systems of service delivery. ... In Haiti's case, these actors [NGOs] were used as a way to circumvent the frustration of working with the government ... this contributed to the establishment of parallel systems of service delivery, eroding legitimacy, capacity and will of the state to deliver key services." The CIDA report goes on to say that, "emphasis on non-governmental actors as development partners also undermined efforts to strengthen good governance."

In fact, the U.S., France and Canada used Haiti's dependence on international funding to precipitate further social disintegration. In 2001, the International Development Bank conceded, "the major factor behind [Haiti's] economic stagnation is the withholding of both foreign grants and loans, associated with the international community's response to the critical political impasse." (At one point, in a desperate bid to comply with international donors, Haiti paid millions of dollars in interest — on loans it had never received.)

Canadian-based NGOs helped the federal government use "development assistance" as a tool of political influence. Around the time of Aristide's second election, the Canadian government began a campaign to actively tie Haitian NGOs to their "aid" money. According to CIDA, the 2000-2002 period "was characterized by a shift in support to civil society." It appears that in the eyes of the Canadian government, "civil society" was in effect equated with opposition to Haiti's elected government. Without exception, documents obtained from CIDA reveal that organizations ideologically opposed to Lavalas were the sole recipients of Canadian government funding. Civil society groups supportive of Lavalas simply did not receive development money. (Ironic, since as a movement of the country's poor, Lavalas supporters should qualify as prime recipients of anti-poverty funding.)

It is amazing to discover the extent to which federal government money was able to "buy" the support of supposedly progressive Canadian organizations and individuals. The full story will not be revealed until all CIDA and other government documents are released, but this is what we've managed to discover so far:

• Several Québec unions received hundreds of thousands of CIDA dollars for work in Haiti through CISO (Centre International de Solidarité Ouvrière) — and were active participants in the Haiti destabilization campaign. In July 2002 the International Confederation of Free Trade Unions (ICFTU) released a statement denouncing, "unjustified continued detention of several trade unionists," a call taken up by a number of Québec unions. The same Québec unions that denounced the Lavalas government have not made amends and have said nothing about the much more severe harassment of Lulu Cherie (next chapter) and other members of the CTH union. Québec unions also worked to dilute an anti-coup resolution proposed by a number of English-Canadian unions to the Canadian Labour Congress convention in Montréal in June 2005.

• In September 2003, Rights and Democracy, an Ottawa-based NGO (all of its money comes from the federal government), formerly headed by the NDP's Ed Broadbent, released a report on Haiti. The report relied heavily upon CIDA employee Philippe Vixamar and the NCHR (see below). The report called the G-184 "grassroots" and a "promising civil society movement" even though it was funded by the International Republican Institute and headed by the country's leading sweatshop owner, Andy Apaid, who had been active in right-wing Haitian politics for many years. (G-184 spokesperson Charles Henry Baker, like Apaid, is white.) CIDA also gave money to some of the G-184 members.

• Three months after the Rights and Democracy report, AQOCI (L'Association Québécoise des Organismes de Coopération Internationale) — a Québec-based network of 54 international development groups — urged the Liberal government to withdraw support from the "Lavalas party regime," and relying upon NCHR, claimed that Aristide's government was "riddled with abuses of human rights."

• The Concertation Pour Haiti (CPH), an informal group of half a dozen NGOs including AQOCI and unions, branded Aristide a "tyrant," his government a "dictatorship," and a "regime of terror" and in mid-February 2004 called for Aristide's removal. This demand was made at the same time CIA-trained thugs swept across the country to depose Aristide. But the CPH's antagonism towards Lavalas wasn't just the by-product of the political upheaval of February. In October 2004 — after months of widespread political repression directed at Lavalas sympathizers — the CPH released a statement blaming the victims. The CPH repeated the claim by Haiti's ruling elite and ultra right that Lavalas launched an "Operation Baghdad" which included beheading police officers. "Operation Baghdad" has been called pro-coup propaganda by numerous observers, designed to divert attention from the de facto government's misdeeds, particularly the murder of at least five peaceful pro-constitution demonstrators on September 30, 2004. In April 2005, the CPH organized a delegation from Haiti to Montréal and Ottawa.

• Yolène Gilles, one of the speakers invited by the CPH, was the coordinator of the "human rights" monitoring program at the National Network for the Defense of Human Rights (RNDDH), formerly known as NCHR (National Coalition for Haitian Rights). NCHR-Haiti, funded by CIDA, changed its name in mid-March 2005 after the parent group in the USA, itself pro-coup, condemned the blatantly partisan work of NCHR-Haiti regarding the imprisonment of constitutional Prime Minister Yvon Neptune. Immediately after the coup, Gilles, a "human rights" worker went on elite-owned radio to name wanted Lavalas "bandits," contributing to a climate of anti-Lavalas terror.

• Another delegate, Danielle Magloire, was a member of the "Council of Wise People" that appointed Latortue as interim prime minister. Latortue's appointment was a blatant violation of Haiti's constitution since the USA, France and Canada created the council after overthrowing the elected government. Magloire's position on the council makes her a direct beneficiary of foreign meddling in Haiti. Her status as a "wise" person came largely from her positions at Enfofanm (Women's info) and Conap, both of which were/are CIDA-funded feminist organizations that would not have grown to prominence without international funding. Coincidentally, Conap is a virulently anti-Lavalas feminist organization that has shunned the language of class struggle in a country where a tiny percent of the population own nearly everything. It is also an organization that has expressed little concern about the dramatic rise in rapes targeting Lavalas sympathizers since the coup. And, demonstrating their commitment to democracy, in mid-July 2005, Magloire's seven-member "Council of Wise People" issued a statement saying any media that gives voice to "bandits" (code for Lavalas supporters) should be shut down. They also asserted that Lavalas should be banned from upcoming elections.

• One result of this cross funding by CIDA of "civil society" organizations was incredible political gymnastics performed to avoid embarrassing the Canadian government. At the CPH press conference mentioned above, Magloire made the absurd claim that Lavalas administered the transition from Aristide to Latortue. Gilles, the "human rights" worker, denied the existence of state-sponsored repression directed at Lavalas, contradicting reports from Amnesty International, The University of Miami, Harvard University, The Institute for Justice and Democracy in Haiti and many others. Gilles' close ties to the de facto government, the UN and Canadian government funding are as well documented as the political repression she denied.

• NCHR-Haiti received $100,000 from CIDA in 2004 for the specific purpose of juridical, medical, psychological, and logistical assistance for victims of an alleged massacre at a town near Saint Marc, called La Scierie. The supposed massacre and NCHR's involvement were put into perspective in a March 9, 2005, article in Haiti-Progrès, which stated: "The illegal government has charged both [former Prime Minister Yvon] Neptune and [former Interior Minister Jocelyn] Privert with involvement in a supposed 'massacre' on February 11, 2004 in St. Marc, an event which reporters and human rights groups almost universally agree never happened. Only the pro-coup U.S.-government-backed National Coalition of Haitian Rights (NCHR) charges that pro-Lavalas partisans slaughtered some 50 people. Pierre Espérance, the NCHR's Haiti bureau chief, says that the remains of the supposed victims were 'eaten by dogs' to explain the absence of any forensic evidence." At the same time that the Canadian embassy in Haiti announced $100,000 for NCHR, an independent report published by the National Lawyers Guild (NLG) laid out NCHR's deficiencies as a human rights organization. The NLG stated that NCHR "could not name a single case in which a Lavalas supporter was a victim," and took the delegation to a room "where the wall was adorned with a large 'wanted' poster featuring Aristide and his cabinet." The April 14, 2004, NLG report concluded: "We condemn the National Coalition for Haitian Rights (NCHR) in Haiti for not maintaining its impartiality as a human rights organization." Despite its partisan politics, NCHR-RNDDH remains the most frequently cited Haitian "human rights" organization by both the international and local (elite-owned) media as well as international NGOs. Largely uncritical of the

Latortue government, NCHR-RNDDH played a crucial role in legitimizing the coup and confusing international public opinion regarding human rights abuses directed against pro-democracy activists. While morgue officials worked overtime, dumping hundreds of bodies (next chapter), NCHR busied themselves with the release of a laudatory report on Latortue's first 45 days in office.

Author and coordinator of the Committee for the Defense of the Haitian People's Rights, Ronald Saint-Jean, documented and analyzed the circumstances surrounding NCHR-RNDDH's role in what he characterizes as the fabrication of the "massacre" in St. Marc. During a tour through Ottawa and Montréal in March of 2005, Saint-Jean denounced Canada's funding of NCHR-RNDDH, informing officials and the press that if Prime Minister Yvon Neptune were to die (there have been at least three close calls while in jail), his blood would be on Canada's hands.

• Canada's involvement in destabilizing the Haitian government included hiring paid agents. The deputy minister of "justice" for the first fifteen months of the interim government, Philippe Vixamar, was on CIDA's payroll for four years up until July 2005 and USAID's payroll for ten years prior to that. He worked under Minister of Justice Bernard Gousse, who was also on USAID's payroll. These two men were in charge of the political portfolio directly responsible for police operations and for all political prisoners in the country. According to the University of Miami investigation: "Vixamar revealed that the United States and Canadian governments play key roles in the justice system in Haiti." The report went on to reveal that Vixamar "stated that he is a political appointee of the Latortue administration, but the Canadian International Development Agency assigned him to this position and is his direct employer."

In 2002, USAID's New Partnerships Initiative described Vixamar as "the coordinator of the Canadian Human Rights Fund in Haiti which is funded ..." by CIDA. Both Vixamar and Gousse were consultants with IFES. (According to the University of Miami human rights report, IFES staff "want to take credit for the ouster of Aristide, but cannot 'out of respect for the wishes of the U.S. Government.'") Researchers for the University of Miami report interviewed Vixamar, who stated that both police activities and the prison system are monitored by NCHR. He added that, "all former militaries are fully vetted by a human rights group [NCHR]" prior to being incorporated into the police force. The report reveals that Vixamar "stated the Ministry of Justice is fully confident in its exclusive reliance on human rights group NCHR to alert it when the police or the Courts commit human rights abuses." In other words, the Canadian-paid deputy justice minister is citing a Canadian-funded "human rights" group to justify or deny abuses such as the illegal imprisonment of Neptune and summary executions carried out by the Haitian police. Canadian officials have refused to discuss Vixamar's role as No. 2 man under Gousse. But, in response to criticism by U.S. Congressman William Delahunt about his ineptitude and corrupt activities as minister of justice, Gousse resigned in June 2005.

• The Canadian government used testimony from NGOs they funded to justify the overthrow of an elected government. On March 25, 2004, representatives from Canadian Catholic Organization for Development and Peace (D&P), the International Centre for Human Rights and Democratic Development (ICHRDD), the International Centre for Legal Resources (ICLR), and Oxfam Québec testified to the Standing Committee on Foreign Affairs and International Trade. With near unanimity, participants accepted the premise that Aristide resigned of his own volition and that Canadian (and international) intervention was entirely justified. Marthe Lapierre of D&P stated that, "We're not talking about a situation where a rebel group suddenly orchestrated Aristide's departure. We're talking about a situation where the Aristide government, since 2000, had gradually lost all legitimacy because of involvement in activities such as serious human rights violations and drug trafficking, but also because it was a profoundly undemocratic government. ... So, we're talking about a government that lost its legitimacy through its own actions." Claiming that Aristide "lost his chance" to negotiate, Lapierre said, "there were OAS resolutions in 2002, that still hadn't been acted on by the Aristide government. At this point, I think he has been given every possible chance to change, and so what we're talking about here is not an armed rebellion, but simply a government that lost its legitimacy by violating human rights." Director of ICHRDD, Jean-Louis Roy applauded Lapierre's analysis, saying, "I don't think Ms. Lapierre's accounting of Haiti's recent history can be challenged." Regional director of Oxfam, Carlos Arancibia, also concurred: "I fully agree with the analysis presented by others. It's important to understand that things went off the rails starting in the year 2000, with the election." Perhaps as compensation, at the end of July 2005, Oxfam Québec received part of two CIDA projects in Haiti worth $15 million.

• As well as managing Haitian civil society the Canadian government also managed the message. It funded Alternatives, a Québec-based media NGO that at time of publication worked with 15 groups in Haiti, all of which were anti-Lavalas. ("Founded in 1994, Alternatives, Action and Communication Network for International Development, is a non-governmental, international solidarity organization" that, also according to its website, receives about 50 percent of its funding from the Canadian government, mostly through CIDA.) Alternatives pays for AlterPresse, the most prominent Francophone online Haitian media outlet and newswire. In April 2005 Alternatives received a share of a $2 million CIDA media project to train Haitian journalists about covering elections — the very elections that Canada hopes will legitimate its role in the February 2004 coup. In a striking illustration of the perils of accepting government funding, an Alternatives supplement in Le Devoir in late June 2005, featured a prominent report that parroted the neoconservative narrative about Haiti. Alternatives' reporting has omitted any mention of political prisoners, violent repression of Lavalas activists, or the basic facts about the coup.

Ottawa-based Haiti solidarity activist Kevin Skerrett summarized the CIDA funding nexus, stating, "This means we have a senior CIDA-funded government official's work being assessed by a CIDA-funded 'human rights' group, whose criticisms just happen to be either absent or muted, which in turn just happens to shield Canada's recent foreign policy in Haiti from criticism." And, we would add, the results are reported on by CIDA-funded media outlets.

AS IF THE CANADIAN connection to NGO-based destabilization wasn't sufficiently disturbing, there has also been extensive military involvement in Haiti, particularly since the overthrow of the elected government and perhaps even before.

The Montréal Gazette's Sue Montgomery revealed on March 9, 2004, that Paul Arcelin (see above) had met in early February of that year with Pierre Pettigrew in Montréal. She wrote, "He took advantage of the visit and the political clout of his sister-in-law [former Conservative MP, Nicole-Arcelin-Roy] to meet with [then-] Health Minister Pierre Pettigrew. ... 'I explained the reality of Haiti to him,' Arcelin said, pulling Pettigrew's business card out of his wallet. 'He promised to make a report to the Canadian government about what I had said.'" Arcelin went on to make even more revealing comments in an interview reported by CanWest News Service, stating that, "Two years ago, I met [rebel leader] Guy Philippe in Santo Domingo and we spent 10 to 15 hours a day together, plotting against Aristide." He continued the interview, stating, "From time to time we'd [Arcelin and Philippe] cross the border clandestinely through the woods to conspire against Aristide, to meet with the opposition and regional leaders to prepare for Aristide's downfall."

Arcelin was a player in both Canada and right wing U.S. circles. In a July 17, 2004, article in Salon, Max Blumenthal wrote: "Others describe more formal ties between IRI and the insurgents. Jean Michel Caroit, chief correspondent in the Dominican Republic for the French daily Le Monde, says he saw [Guy] Philippe's political advisor, Paul Arcelin, at an IRI meeting at Hotel Santo Domingo in December 2003. Caroit, who was having drinks in the lobby with several attendees, said the meeting was convened 'quite discreetly.' His account dovetailed with that of a Haitian journalist who told Salon on condition of anonymity that Arcelin often attended IRI meetings in Santo Domingo as Convergence's representative to the Dominican Republic."

Arcelin would also prove prophetic. An AFP article on March 2, 2004: "Paul Arcelin, who serves as 'coordinator' for the insurgency led by Guy Philippe, told a cheering crowd across from the presidential palace, that the rebels would detain Neptune, a close Aristide ally, for him to be tried for unspecified crimes." Fearing assassination and certain of his innocence, Neptune gave himself over to authorities. To the day this book was published he languished in prison despite repeated international calls for his release and no formal charges against him.

On March 19, 2004, Latortue heralded as "freedom fighters" the convicted human rights violators and drug dealers who helped overthrow the elected government. The special representative of the OAS and head of the OAS special mission to Haiti, Canadian diplomat David Lee, stood next to Latortue when he made this statement and did not object.

Five hundred Canadian soldiers backed the Latortue regime between March and August 2004 and did little to disarm the paramilitaries. In Petionville, the former military maintained a base and openly wielded high-powered weapons a year after the coup. Three months after the coup, the Haiti Accompaniment Project stated, "The UN military command in the north coordinates its activities with Guy Philippe, the rebel leader who is responsible for major human rights violations — including assassinations — in the period preceding the coup." As this book went to press, Philippe, who has established a political party and will run for president, functioned unimpeded at his party headquarters in Cap-Haïtien.

In January 2005 the installed regime offered each of the 5,000-8,000 ex-soldiers "back pay" of $3,000 US; the UN chipped in over $2.8 million. At the end of March 2005, MINUSTAH (the UN force) commander Juan Gabriel Valdés lobbied the UN for another $40 million to be added to the $29 million already budgeted by Latortue for the reformation of the disbanded army — an astounding sum when one considers that in 2002 total government expenditures were $300 million. To receive the initial funding the soldiers were not required to disarm.

It is unclear whether any Canadian "aid" went directly to these former soldiers. Quite clear, however, is that by June 2005 Canada had given over $100 million to Haiti, about the same as the U.S., which has an economy ten times as big. Directly or indirectly, western countries provided Latortue with money to buy off the hoodlums that helped him to power.

The presence of a non-elected Latortue government also loosened the pocketbooks of international financiers. The World Bank announced in mid January 2005 that it would release $73 million to the installed government. But for Haiti to receive this money it had to pay $52 million in outstanding debt. Canada stepped in to give the regime a $12.7 million grant. A July 2004 Washington donors' conference announced $1.2 billion in aid, $180 million of which was to come from Canada. The International Development Bank, which at the request of the U.S. withheld hundreds of millions of dollars from the elected Lavalas government for three years, announced in March 2005 that it would release $270 million to the de facto government. The World Bank reopened its Port-au-Prince office, which had been closed for ten years. All this contrasts with the position of Canada, the U.S. and the European Union to stop aid to the Haitian government due to opposition accusations that the May 2000 elections were "unfair." The interim government did not win an "unfair" election, because it was not elected at all. It completely failed any test of democratic legitimacy, having been installed by foreign powers. Further proof of its illegitimacy was its support for the reinstatement of the notoriously brutal and anti-democratic Haitian army.

Directly recreating the army so soon after the coup would not have looked good, so the police force was expanded to include many former soldiers. Individuals with a military background made up 85 percent of the first class of post-coup police academy graduates. Five hundred former members of the Haitian army were integrated into the police force, with plans for an additional 500-1,000 former soldiers to be hired by the start of 2006. While the Haiti Accompaniment Project was in Haiti, then de facto minister of the interior, former general Herard Abraham, "issued a public call for former military living overseas to submit their files to the Ministry of Interior for consideration." Already in March 2005, Reuters reported that, "only one of the top-12 police commanders in the Port-au-Prince area does not have a military background, and most regional police chiefs are also ex-soldiers." The military is effectively being reconstituted, with help from some violent folk from abroad.

The U.S. also chipped in thousands of new weapons for the police. After lifting a thirteen-year arms embargo against Haiti, by April 2005 the Bush administration had, according to the Geneva-based Small Arms Survey, sold some $7 million worth of arms to the installed government. (The U.S. government disputes this figure.) In a

June 2005 ceremony attended by U.S. Assistant-Secretary of State Roger Noriega and Canada's Denis Coderre, the HNP were presented with over $2 million dollars worth of military/policing equipment. This provoked passage in the U.S. House of Representatives of a bill to ban such shipments. Said Congresswoman Barbara Lee, who introduced the amendment, "The United States must not be complicit in helping to arm criminals and human rights abusers." At press time, the U.S. Senate had not yet ratified the bill.

Canada was also directly involved in the process of reintegrating ex-soldiers into the police force. In addition to the approximately 100 Canadian police officers in Haiti, the entire 1,600-member UN civilian police force (CIVPOL) was led by David Beer of the RCMP. There were also members of the Canadian Forces in the command structure of the UN military contingent. Beer was previously in Iraq assisting counterinsurgency efforts and in his CIVPOL role worked closely with the Haitian police. CIVPOL's main job was, in fact, to train and assist the HNP — the same police responsible for political prisoners and assassinations taking place almost daily. There were reports that Canadian Joint Task Force Two (JTF2) soldiers were still secretly in Haiti in mid-2005. This information was impossible to confirm since the Canadian government refuses to disclose the whereabouts of the JTF2, but it was corroborated by a number of sources. Furthermore, Claude Rochon, former chief of police in Montréal, led the efforts of Canadian private "security experts" CANPOL, to help formulate "strategic planning" for the HNP. Rochon engaged in similar efforts as part of Canada's intervention in post-9/11 Afghanistan.

According to UN Security Council resolution 1542, MINUSTAH is "to assist the transitional government in monitoring, restructuring and reforming the Haitian National Police consistent with democratic policing standards, including through the vetting and certification of its personnel, advising on its reorganization and training." While the UN resolution sounds okay on paper it means something different on the ground. Harvard University Law Student Advocates for Human Rights investigators reported that "MINUSTAH's most visible efforts have involved providing logistical support to police operations, which … are implicated in human rights abuses, such as arbitrary arrest and detention and extra-judicial killings." A resident of Bel Air told the Harvard investigators that "every time the HNP wants to kill or arrest people, they send in MINUSTAH first." UN General Augusto Heleno Pereira more or less confirmed the Bel Air resident's claim, stating "we offered the police the protection they didn't have. We give space for the HNP to operate, yes, we do."

It was difficult to ascertain specifics on CIVPOL/ HNP operations as Canadian officials refused requests for this information. A CIVPOL unit commander from Québec City, however, told Thomas Griffin, lead author of the university of Miami Law School report, that he "engage[d] in daily guerilla warfare." At press time, HNP Chief Léon Charles and CIVPOL head Beer would both publicly refer to the "urban war" that is being waged.

CARLO DADE, SENIOR ADVISOR for the CIDA-funded FOCAL, on April 1, 2004 told the Foreign Affairs standing committee: "The U.S. would welcome Canadian involve-ment and Canada's taking the lead in Haiti. The admin-istration in Washington has its hands more than full with Afghanistan, Iraq and the potential in Korea and the Mideast. There is simply not the ability to concentrate ... But it's a sign of the interest and openness in the United States to have Canada take a lead on this." Canadian action was justified on the grounds that, compared to the U.S. and France, Canada's reputation is not too bad in Haiti, allowing them to "get away" with more.

Canada has contributed significantly to the dismantling of Haiti's democratic government and has unquestionably aligned itself with Haiti's traditional colonial powers — France and the USA. These were the three countries cited when Brazilian commander of the UN mission, General

Augusto Heleno Ribeiro, told a congressional commission in Brazil in early 2005 that "we are under extreme pressure from the international community to use violence." These three countries pressed for stronger measures against "gangs" — not the armed paramilitary thugs — supporters of Aristide living in the slums of Port-au-Prince. With the July 2005 reports of direct UN forces involvement in massacres (see below), it looks like Canada, the USA and France got their way.

The Canadian government is also at the forefront of promoting "protectorate status" for Haiti. This arrangement was on the agenda at the Ottawa Initiative meeting thirteen months before the coup. Former Canadian minister for La Francophonie and Latin America, Denis Paradis, was a proponent of the "Responsibility-to-Protect" doctrine, a neocolonial policy that argues powerful countries must "protect" weak countries whenever it is perceived necessary. According to Paradis, the responsibility-to-protect doctrine means that, "when we're in a situation like Haiti, for example, people should try to settle the whole thing with the government... after that if, it doesn't work ... they don't exclude the military taking over a country where the state failed to protect its people. You have around the world some leaders that are in this situation. It's a new concept ... So, it's the responsibility of the international community to act and I do believe that even if you say that they passed a resolution at the UN the day after Aristide [was removed] ... even if Aristide didn't leave at the time, they should have asked the UN to take the case of Haiti further." Certainly the Canadian government appears prepared to take Haiti further.

According to a FOCAL plan for Haiti's future, commissioned by Parliament's foreign affairs committee, the country's different ministries would fall under Canadian oversight. Québec's ministry of education, for instance, would oversee Haiti's education system, which some say is the reason Jean Charest made the first ever trip by a Québec premier to Haiti in June 2005. (Paul Martin made the first ever trip by a Canadian prime minister to Haiti in November 2004) The FOCAL plan puts Haiti's environment ministry under Canadian federal government supervision. Contrary to what Paradis may claim, colonialism is not a new concept.

CANADA IN HAITI   71

4 / A Human Rights Disaster

THE HAITIAN PEOPLE have endured many periods of widespread human rights violations, notably under the regimes of Papa and Baby Doc Duvalier and the military junta following the first U.S.-backed coup against Aristide, when thousands were murdered. While no one would claim that the period of democracy from 1995-2004 was perfect, even if one believed the wildest allegations of Lavalas critics, the situation for the vast majority of Haitians improved dramatically. But since the overthrow of the president, and over five thousand elected officials, there has been a quantitative and qualitative leap in human rights abuses.

"THEY VIOLATED ME. [When it was happening] I closed my eyes and waited for them to finish ... One of the men told me to open my eyes and look at him while he [raped me]. I didn't want to look at him. They hit me when I cried." Marjory was a 14-year-old from Cap Haïtien whose father was a local trade unionist. He was forced into hiding following the coup and the disbanded soldiers, looking for him, raped Marjory, her mother and an 11 year-old cousin. According to attorney Mario

HAITIAN NATIONAL POLICE: Raids by HNP regularly target Lavalas supporters in poor neighborhoods.

Joseph from Bureau des Avocats Internationaux (BAI), "rape is becoming a common tool of oppression. ... Women and young girls are raped because their father or another relative is a member of Lavalas or is targeted [by the political opposition]. They are raped as a form of punishment. The victims do not feel they can go to the police for help with their problems because in many areas the people who victimized them are the ones running the show; they are the ones patrolling the streets as if they are police, committing crimes with impunity under the eyes of the UN."

IT'S IMPOSSIBLE TO ASCERTAIN how many have died from political violence and repression since the coup. But honest human rights investigations, carried out by groups with limited resources, show a consistent pattern. A U.S. National Lawyers Guild delegation visiting Haiti shortly after the coup reported that on March 7, 2004, morgue officials dumped 800 bodies and another 200 three weeks later. (This is an extraordinary number in light of a morgue worker's report that the average is under 100 bodies per month.) A fact-finding mission carried out by the Harvard University Law Student Advocates for Human Rights quoted Canadian police officers in December 2004 as "not being interested" in investigating credible reports of mass graves containing victims of political violence. An Institute for Justice and Democracy in Haiti (IJDH) report, covering the period until the end of May 2004, documented (including pictures) about 100 murders, mainly targeted at Lavalas supporters. A human rights report by the University of Miami School of Law Center for the Study of Human Rights, covering the period November 11-21 2004, confirmed the brutality of the installed regime: "After ten months under an interim government backed by the United States, Canada, and France and buttressed by a United Nations force, Haiti's people churn inside a hurricane of violence. Gunfire crackles, once bustling streets are abandoned to cadavers, and whole neighborhoods are cut off from the outside world.

AFTERMATH OF UN RAID: Many houses in the poor neighborhood of Cité Soleil were destroyed by "peacekeepers."

Nightmarish fear now accompanies Haiti's poorest in their struggle to survive in destitution. Gangs, police, irregular soldiers, and even UN peacekeepers bring fear." The Harvard University investigation documented a number of disturbing deaths during trips to Haiti in October 2004 and January 2005. High-level World Bank memos contain references to "thousands" of Haitians killed in the political violence since Aristide's ouster.

A human rights delegation sponsored by the San Francisco Labor Council reported that residents of a poor Port-au-Prince neighborhood claimed to have seen 23 bodies after a UN forces raid to kill "gang leader" Dread

KILLED BY UN TROOPS: Four-year-old Stanley Romelus was shot in the head during raid July 6, 2005, according to his father.

Wilme in the early morning of July 6, 2005. Residents of Cité Soleil said UN forces shot out electric transformers in their neighborhood. People were killed in their homes and on the street as they went to work. According to journalists and eyewitnesses, one man named Léon Cherry, age 46, was shot and killed on his way to work for a flower company. Another man, Mones Belizaire, was shot as he readied for work in a local sweatshop and died later from an infection. An unidentified street vendor was shot in the head and killed instantly. One man was shot in his ribs while brushing his teeth. Another was shot in the jaw as he left his house to make some money to pay his wife's medical costs

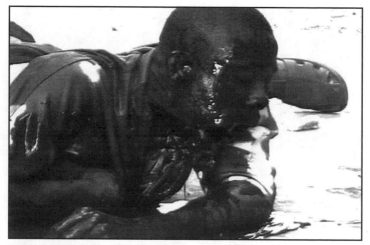

LEONCE CHERY: The 31-year-old man is shown in this print from video moments after being shot in the jaw by UN troops.

and endured a slow death. Yet another man named Mira was shot and killed while urinating in his home. A mother, Sena Romelus, and her two young children were killed in their home, either by bullets or by an 83-CC grenade thrown by UN forces. A Reuters story quoted a spokesperson from Médecins Sans Frontieres (MSF, Doctors Without Borders) saying they treated more than two dozen people that day, including a pregnant woman who survived surgery but lost her baby. "We received 27 people wounded by gunshots on July 6. Three quarters were children and women," said Ali Besnaci, head of the MSF in Haiti. "We had not received so many wounded in one day for a long time." A UN military spokesman, Col. Elouafi Boulbars, said UN troops killed five "criminals" during the operation. But after those bodies were taken away, a Reuters TV crew filmed seven other bodies of people killed during the operation, including those of two one-year-old baby boys and a woman in her 60s. Eyewitnesses claimed that the offensive overwhelmed the community and that there was not a "firefight," but rather a slaughter. Primarily UN forces conducted the operation, with the HNP taking a back seat, according to witnesses. Some reports had as many as 80 people killed.

Associated Press reported on April 27, 2005: "Police fired on protesters demanding the release of detainees loyal to Haiti's ousted president Wednesday, killing at least five demonstrators, UN officials and witnesses said. Witnesses said Haitian police arrived as the demonstrators neared the headquarters of the UN peacekeeping mission in the capital of Port-au-Prince and fired shots to disperse the crowd ... The incident marked the third time in three months that Haitian police have fatally opened fire on demonstrators in Port-au-Prince."

Independent Haiti-based U.S. journalist Kevin Pina reported that on October 15, 2004, "the General Hospital had to call the Ministry of Health today in order to demand emergency vehicles to remove the more than 600 corpses that have been stockpiled there, that have been coming

CANADIAN POLICE: Citizens have a right to ask what exactly their civil servants are doing in Haiti.

in from the killing over the last two weeks alone." Noted human rights reporter Cesar Chelala would later repeat these numbers in the Japan Times on March 21, 2005. A week after Pina`s report, the state morgue was declared off limits, except to visitors pre-approved by the General Hospital administrator. Interviewing morgue officials in mid-November, University of Miami investigators discovered "that since September 30, 2004 ... the HNP rarely even bring people killed by violence to the morgue. They stated that the police simply take the bodies of those they kill directly to undisclosed dumping grounds, sometimes stopping by the morgue only to borrow the dump truck."

Based on mounting anecdotal evidence, it is conservative to assume no less than another thousand people were killed through summer 2005, in addition to those tallied in the morgue reports in the month following the coup.

During a pro-Lavalas demonstration on September 30, 2004, the HNP fired into a crowd of some 10,000 protestors. Several unarmed demonstrators were killed or wounded under the watchful eye of UN peacekeepers. The day after these killings, the installed Prime Minister Latortue was quoted saying: "We shot them, some of them fell, others were injured, others ran away." Pro-Lavalas demonstrators were blamed for the violence, though no meaningful evidence was offered. In post-coup Haiti the victims are always guilty.

On December 1, 2004, two weeks after the government had fired more than a dozen experienced prison guards, a riot broke out at the heavily fortified national penitentiary. At first the government claimed seven prisoners were killed. This number was later increased to 10, but subsequent investigations by Reuters, the London Observer and the IJDH suggest that this was a gross underestimate. The actual number of those who lost their lives is likely three or four times that reported and, according to the IJDH, could be as high as 110. Authorities did their best to prevent prisoners from talking to the outside world. Three weeks after the massacre, the downtown Port-au-Prince prison

WANTED POSTER: Names and pictures of Lavalas supporters are put up on police station walls. The people often then "disappear."

was still off limits to family members and most outsiders. Eight months after the incident, the UN had yet to release its inquiry into the events. The interim Haitian government admitted that of the 1,100 people held in the prison when the riot occurred, less than 20 had been convicted of any crime. Hundreds of detainees who languish in overcrowded cells are Lavalas activists. Among those still in prison at press time were the elected Interior Minister Jocelerme Privert and Prime Minister Neptune.

CANADIAN POLICE OFFICER: About 100 Canadian police and army personnel were still in Haiti in summer 2005.

HAITI WAS NEITHER WITHOUT violence nor poverty prior to the coup. It was insecure and impoverished, with a gross domestic product 40 percent smaller than Nicaragua, the second poorest country in the hemisphere. Most institutions that existed were fragile and prone to mismanagement. In an attempt to dismiss concerns over political prisoners, former Canadian minister of the francophonie, Denis Paradis pointed out that, "half of the people that were in jail in Haiti, we're talking a couple of years ago now, didn't have any file on them; they couldn't find why they are in jail."

It is true that well before the coup Haiti's justice system was weak, corrupt and repressive. Well before the coup, some Lavalas officials were part of the problem. A number had cars and houses impossible to afford on a public official's salary. Some were stealing from the state. Some were involved in the drug trade. While deplorable, this corruption pales in comparison to the 1991-94 military dictatorship or to the time of "Baby Doc", who makes the all-time top-ten list of international embezzlers.

In a country where the total government budget is little more than $300 million US — $30 million for the police, courts and justice system — and drug traffickers spend more than $75 million annually in bribes, according to U.S. State Department figures reported by the New York Times March 9, 2004, it is no surprise that corruption was widespread. It is surprising, however, that more than a year after overthrowing the allegedly corrupt Aristide, the Latortue administration was unable to offer any proof linking the elected president to the alleged corruption. If evidence were available, Latortue's administration would have made it public. Perhaps the subject makes the installed prime minister a little uncomfortable; many close to Latortue were themselves entangled in corruption scandals within months of his taking power. For example, his nephew Youri, head of Latortue's security detail, has been dubbed "Mr. 30 percent" by the French press for the cut he allegedly takes on drug deals. The authors have also uncovered his involvement in kidnappings and illegal weapons deals. The International Crisis Group has also noted that whereas drug dealers with Lavalas connections are being targeted for arrest by the DEA, others, such as Youri Latortue are being left untouched. In July 2005, Gérard Latortue admitted that 6,000 paychecks were being issued to police officer when there were only 4,000 of them. Fifty percent of the salaries were somehow being drained from Haiti's meager treasury.

ARRIVING BY BUS FROM the Dominican Republic in December 2004, our host failed to pick us up. Fortunately we had Lulu's phone number and he with his wife, Ginette Apollon, quickly arrived at the depot to give us a lift. Paul Lulu Chery, a big, congenial man, was general coordinator of the CTH (Coordination des Travailleurs Haitiens) union federation. As Lulu drove us to our destination he calmly told us how the police went to their house two months earlier demanding to know his whereabouts. Ginette, President of the National Commission of Women Workers

RETURN TO DEMOCRACY: Many demonstrations such as this one in Port-au-Prince have been attacked by police.

(CNFT), who was home at the time, interjected in a more outraged manner. "They told me if Lulu didn't report to the police station by 6 p.m. the next day, I would find his body in the street." Lulu went into hiding for a month and was concerned that his teenage son and daughter could find themselves without a father. Still, he refused to cease his union activities. The installed government also harassed other members of the CTH, the largest union federation in the country, according to Lulu and Ginette. The IJDH reported that on September 16, 2004, "police officers raided the offices of the Confederation of Haitian Workers labour union and arrested nine union members, all without a warrant. The official justification for the arrest was that the defendants were 'close to the Lavalas authorities.'" In mid-April 2005 Ginette attended the Encuentro Mundial de Solidaridad Con la Revolucion Bolivariana in Venezuela, invited by INAMUJER, a Venezuelan women's rights organization. Upon returning she was interrogated and Lulu was also harassed by police at the airport. They claimed Ginette received funds to buy weapons for Lavalas. Little money was found, but Ginette, who suffers from high blood pressure, was hospitalized.

SEMERESTE BOLIÈRE WAS THE elected mayor of Petit Goave, a town of 15,000 in the south west of Haiti. Arrested in March 2004 by the new authorities, he escaped and went into hiding in the capital. Sipping cola from a '50s-style bottle in a run-down city centre labour hall, Bolière said he was forced from office in Petit Goave by former military officers who led the rebellion. Also seated with us was Ronald St Jean, a human rights activist who echoed Bolière's conviction that throughout the country, hundreds if not thousands of elected mayors, council members and senators had been forced into hiding or exile. They argued that the officials who managed to salvage their positions had made accommodations with the U.S.-armed paramilitary thugs, many known drug runners and others convicted murderers. St Jean and Bolière expressed deep disappointment about Canadian involvement in the undermining of Haitian democracy.

IN THE PERIOD FOLLOWING the 2004 coup, social projects identified with Lavalas became a target. The U.S. Marines, who occupied a new medical school that the Aristide Foundation had built to train doctors in under-serviced areas, set the tone. As of the printing of this book, the UN continued to occupy the school and the installed government announced in late June 2005 that it was "freezing" a million dollars from the university "linked to Aristide." About 300 medical students were unable to resume classes, a catastrophe in a country with less than two thousand doctors, 90 percent of whom practise in the capital.

The day after Aristide's removal, Transport Plus, a highly successful bus co-operative subsidized by the Lavalas government, had most of its 200 buses torched. The government literacy program, a Lavalas initiative, fell apart under the Latortue regime, depriving thousands of their education. Subsidies for schoolchildren

KIDS AT SCHOOL: One of the great achievements of the Lavalas government was the opening of many new schools.

and schoolbooks were also eliminated. Terror swept the countryside as former soldiers assumed power. Politically active peasants were killed and land reform reversed in favor of former landowners, a situation particularly intense in the Artibonite Valley. Peasants in Haiti face a return to feudal-like conditions.

In the weeks after the coup, 4 p.m. was a particularly tense time in the capital because at that hour the names of alleged Lavalas "bandits" were read over the (elite-controlled) radio stations, forcing hundreds into hiding.

BEFORE THE FEBRUARY 2004 UPHEAVAL Rea Dol, a 38-year-old mother of three, worked for the District of Petionville, an upscale suburb of Port-au-Prince. When the "interim" government installed Marie Renée, a new non-elected mayor, Dol found herself out of work. Still owed back wages, she was fired with neither cause nor compensation. Dol said she was just one of thousands — more than 2,000 at the state telecom company alone — laid off for their perceived political affiliation.

As we enjoyed a lunch of rice and chicken, Dol vented her frustration over unemployment lines in a country where most of the urban population is looking for work and social assistance does not exist. She noted that many of the recently unemployed, especially the hundreds of purged police officers, had taken to crime. Some have probably become "Chimères" — a type of "gang" that eludes exact definition — "pro-Aristide" groups that the media claim are behind the growing violence.

Dol became distraught as she discussed the rising cost of food staples, rice and beans — another factor that has driven many to lawlessness. Food importation

SPEAKING TRUTH: 10,000 march in Cap Haïtien behind a banner that claims 'Operation Baghdad' is a G-184 plot to demonize Lavalas.

is controlled by a handful of wealthy families, who were antagonistic to Aristide's price-stabilizing policies and supported his removal.

Since the coup, many staples have doubled in price. Berthony F. A. Mercier, a 50-year-old Port-au-Prince sign painter put it succinctly to the New York Times, stating that "the people who sell the rice are the people who kicked Aristide out."

A rise in malnutrition has undoubtedly taken place, but amidst the chaos who is keeping track?

SINCE THE COUP, THOUSANDS of Haitians have fled political persecution to the Dominican Republic or elsewhere. Tens of thousands more have been driven out of the country by the worsening security and economic conditions. U.S. Coast Guard officials boasted in Congressional hearings about the thousands of Haitians prevented from even getting in the water. "Operation ABLE SENTRY blanketed the coastline of Haiti with legacy Coast Guard Deepwater assets, which interdicted more than 1,000 illegal migrants during this operation and deterred many thousands more from taking to sea in unsafe boats." The Dominican Republic, where more than a million Haitians live, has begun the forced mass repatriation of Haitian migrants; human rights groups have referred to this practice as "ethnic genocide."

THE LATE 1980s SAW the founding of Lafanmi Selavi, an orphanage for street children initiated by Aristide. In a disturbing turn of events, Aristide's identification with street kids proved deadly to many of the tens of thousands living without parents in Port-au-Prince. A missionary who works with street children, who asked that her name not be used, told Lyn Duff of Pacific News

Service, "I only saw three murdered [homeless] children between 1995 and the beginning of 2004." Yet, "since Feb. 29, I have seen or heard of over 150 murders of street children and have personally witnessed the attacks on more than a dozen occasions."

Former street child Lolo Reagan told the Haiti Information Project that "the police are in the habit of landing in the spots where the children live in the middle of the night and then of proceeding to arrest them, and killing them." Michael Brewer, director of Haiti Street Kids Inc., confirmed the deaths saying that military patrols in Port-au-Prince are known to kill street children "for sport."

JUST BEFORE CHRISTMAS 2004, inside the women's Petionville prison, we met two prominent political prisoners, internationally acclaimed folk music singer, So Anne (Annette Auguste) and the former head of the Haitian Senate, Yvon Feuille. A feisty 63-year-old, So Anne has brought the music of Haiti to the world. Also a political organizer, she is committed to improving the lives of ordinary people in the poorest country of the Americas. Maintaining a cheerful disposition, she told us about being behind bars, without charge, since May 10, 2004, when U.S. marines barged into her home in the dead of night, killings two dogs and arresting everyone, including several children who were also blindfolded. Seven months later, So Anne remained defiant. She flexed her arm muscles and repeatedly bellowed, "they won't intimidate me, they won't intimidate me." Several international appeals have been made for the release of So Anne who, at press time remained resilient, but in jail.

HAITI'S PRISONS ARE SQUALID, intimidating and a violation of human rights. The University of Miami report documents one example of 42 prisoners being kept in a nine-feet by nine-feet cell for as long as thirty days. The UN offered Latortue's government more than $50,000 to improve conditions, but prison authorities refused the money.

This prompted Jacques Dyotte, head of the UN program for the reformation of Haiti's penitentiary system, to resign from his position in November 2004. He cited the government's lack of interest in improving prison conditions as a reason for his departure. "It was worse than I have ever seen," said Dyotte, who had been on the job since July 2000.

While the prisons are full of Lavalas activists, (700 in the capital alone, according to the Catholic Church's Justice and Peace Commission) drug dealers, rapists, murderers and human rights violators roam free. During the overthrow of constitutional order, rebels made sure to empty prisons throughout the country — at least half the former prisoners are thought to still be on the loose.

THE HUMAN RIGHTS SITUATION was so bad 16 months after the overthrow of the elected government that the "head of UN peacekeeping operations says conditions in parts of Haiti are worse than in Sudan's devastated Darfur region," according to a June 28, 2005, Voice of America report.

"A month ago I was in Darfur, and God knows the situation of the IDPs [internally displaced persons] there is tragic, but at least, thanks to the mobilization of the international community, you see IDPs in camps in al Fasher or cities in Darfur, they have medical facilities, there is drinking water, there are latrines. It's a terrible situation, but some of the basics are being provided by the international community. The Haitians in Cap Haïtien, this is a quiet place, they have no drinking water, no latrines, garbage not collected, situation is squalor, its terrible. They are in [a] worse situation than some of the IDPs I saw in Darfur," said Undersecretary-General for Peacekeeping Jean-Marie Guehenno.

Guehenno added that Sudan's Darfur region is considered the world's worst humanitarian disaster. He may even have correctly diagnosed the source of the problem — an illegitimate government — "So long as you don't have an effective law and order structure that is trusted by people, seen as fair, impartial, has basic means to deliver law and order, you need an international presence there." In other words, when armed thugs (foreign or domestic) overthrow a popularly elected government, human rights abuses are an inevitable result.

5 / Why? Destabilization as a Tool of the Rich and Powerful

IRAQ HAS OIL, BUT what is wanted from Haiti? On the surface it doesn't appear to be worth much to Canada, France or the United States, yet all three states expended resources removing the elected president and government. Haiti's value or importance may not be obvious at first, but what is clear is that none of the countries paid much of a political price. The limited popular outcry means destabilizing Haiti has thus far come at an insignificant cost to these governments.

To understand why Haiti was destabilized, one must look at the economic and ideological driving forces of imperialism. From the slavery, racism and colonization of hundreds of years ago to the racism and neoliberal agenda of today, Western powers have worked ceaselessly and diligently to prevent the former slave republic from realizing the great promise of its independence.

Anyone in doubt about whether or not Aristide was kowtowing enough to the neoliberal world order need only look at the World Bank's reaction to Aristide's latest ouster. Already, in exchange for a $61 million loan, the World Bank is requiring "public-private partnership and governance in the education and health sectors," according to bank documents. In a startling document at the end of 2004, the World Bank/International Development Assistance Program stated: "The transition period and the Transitional Government provide a window of opportunity for implementing economic governance reforms with the involvement of civil society stakeholders that may be hard for a future government to undo."

The U.S. reinforced the World Bank's rather blatant position in its "principles of engagement in Haiti." According to U.S. Assistant Secretary of State for Latin America Roger Noriega, the U.S. position was to encourage "the Government of Haiti to move forward, at the appropriate time, with restructuring and privatization of some public sector enterprises." Noriega explicitly called for the privatization of Haiti's ports. The World Bank also indicated that Haiti's state run telecommunications company, TELECO, should be privatized. A May 2005 World Bank report showed that Canada was overseeing the "decentralization" and management of Haiti's electrical system.

With Aristide out of the picture, the interim government, in lockstep with the foreign powers and elements of the Haitian diaspora, planned to fast track this neoliberal stranglehold. Western elites seem intolerant to resistance of any kind and Aristide was perceived as a barrier to a complete implementation of the neoliberal agenda.

The attitude seems to have been, "If we can't force our way in Haiti, where can we?"

The installed government pledged to adhere to numerous structural reforms, including the "potential" privatization of five major industries — a move Aristide previously refused. In an interview that appeared in an August 2005 issue of Nation magazine, Aristide told journalist Naomi Klein that the U.S. was furious with what it perceived as an unfulfilled promise to privatize several state companies. Following Aristide's 1994 return, division over further privatizations led to a split within Lavalas and the creation of Fanmi Lavalas. The Lavalas government had become ambivalent about further privatizations after the U.S. and international credit institutions pressed for the selling of the national cement company in 1997. Purchased by one of Haiti's wealthiest citizens, Gilbert Bigio, the company fetched $9 million, despite a potential annual profit of $20-30 million US. Following other economic advice from international credit agencies was equally disadvantageous.

The promotion of low-wage sweatshops was one specific economic motivation for the 2004 coup. During a December 2004 trip to Haiti, Colin Powell repeatedly plugged the Haiti Economic Recovery Opportunity in an interview with elite-owned Radio Metropole: "We have the HERO Act before Congress now ... We would like to see the Act passed and I will be examining and discussing it this week with our Congress."

The act would give duty-free treatment for apparel items assembled in Haiti if that country makes progress towards "a market-based economy that protects private property rights, incorporates an open rules-based trading system, and minimizes government interference in the economy through measures such as price controls, subsidies, and government ownership of economic assets" and "the elimination of barriers to United States trade and investment." The act also requires that Haiti "does not engage in activities that undermine United States national security or foreign policy interests."

Canadian officials seemed to wholeheartedly endorse transforming Haiti into a land that is good for business — our business. At press time, Canadian mining companies KWG Resources and St. Geneviève Resources were waiting to exploit an anticipated five billion pounds of copper in a Haitian deposit. These companies, in partnership with a Haitian businessman, will have unfettered access to a further 522,000 tonnes of gold ore. Several hundred million dollars in profits were waiting below Haitian soil (and under the feet of farmers) for exploitation.

Montréal-based Gildan Activewear announced plans to move part of its controversial Honduran El Progresso plant to Haiti to escape accountability for workers' rights violations. With a massive warehouse in North Carolina and as owner of 40 percent of the U.S. T-shirt market, Gildan would benefit from the HERO act were it implemented. Gildan employs up to 5,000 people in Port-au-Prince's assembly sector, including work subcontracted to Andy Apaid, the leader of the G-184.

In addition to the interests of specific companies, Haiti's low wages serve a broader corporate purpose — they provide ammunition to employers throughout the Americas who can point to Haiti's example in the event that workers in Mexico or Jamaica try to improve their lot. "We could always move to Haiti," is the warning refrain that confronts workers' struggles. The Haitian populace has been pushed to the very depths of "the race to the bottom" unleashed by neoliberal globalization, to the extent that it might accurately be renamed "the race to Haiti." Foreign investors and Haiti's sweatshop-owning elite are working hard to keep it that way. Needless to say, Lavalas' doubling of the minimum wage in 2003 wasn't popular in business circles. It was similarly not appreciated in 1995 or 1991.

Yet the antagonism of the Haitian elite towards Aristide goes beyond disdain at raising the minimum wage. Haiti's "morally repugnant elite," as a U.S. ambassador once put it, feared the Lavalas government's moves towards empowering the poor majority. In a society where a large percentage of the population is deemed sub-human, electoral slogans such as Lavalas' "tout moun se moun" [all people are people] are subversive.

The disdain for the poor is palatable. In Haiti's caste-like system there is fear among the elite about the poor. For a long time the elite successfully repressed the culture of the peasants and slum dwellers. Aristide eliminated the designation on birth certificates — moun andeyo (outsiders) — for people born outside of Port-au-Prince. To the dismay of the Christian establishment, the government decided to recognize baptisms, marriages and funerals performed by voodoo officials in May of 2003. Another historical source of elite control continues to be the marginalization of Creole, spoken by 90 percent of the population. The 10 percent who speak French were threatened by the elevation of the language because government jobs, traditionally the preserve of French speakers, could then go to speakers of Creole.

The educational achievements of the Lavalas government were considerable. More schools were built under Lavalas governments from 1994-2004 than in the first 190 years of Haitian history, reversing a shockingly poor educational system where up until 1985 there was only one secondary school for every thirty-five prisons. Lavalas' literacy programs helped thousands of adults, driving illiteracy down from around 80 percent to 50 percent across the country. Despite sustained popularity among the poor, most of these programs were abolished after February 29, 2004. The coup attempted to sweep away the small steps in the direction of an empowered majority.

An elite fury brewed over Aristide's ability to mobilize the masses and the poor's growing sense of empowerment and entitlement. Then in 1995 Aristide disbanded the army — without a military the wealthy no longer had an internal force to protect their interests and property in the event of popular mobilization. Haiti's army never fought a foreign army. Its sole purpose was to suppress the internal population. In the countryside a system of over 500 section chiefs, appendages of the army, controlled the population through force. In Port-au-Prince the army was the overseer of government, as demonstrated in Aristide's 1991 overthrow. Not surprising, the army is widely reviled in Haiti and many on the international scene applauded its demise. Yet those now in control desire its resurrection. The island on which Haiti is situated is shared by the Dominican Republic, whose military helped to train the disbanded Haitian army. It is in the interest of the Dominican army for Haiti to have a military force because it provides justification for the Dominican army's existence and sustenance. Haiti has been the enemy for two hundred years of Dominican history.

Of more significance is the U.S. interest in the recreation of the Haitian military, which has been the tool of choice in many interventions. This peculiar relationship extends back to 1915-34, during the popular Cacao uprising against U.S. occupation. To suppress the revolt, U.S. forces, through an act of Congress, organized and consolidated an armed force, which resulted in the creation of the modern Haitian army. The U.S. maintained its influence over the Haitian army into the 1990s and in 1991 the generals that overthrew Aristide were trained and funded by the CIA.

U.S. involvement in Haiti is further explained through a geopolitical understanding of the region. Haiti occupies a valuable location on the globe with a dazzling view. Not far away is Venezuela, making it a good spot for Bush to keep an eye on President Hugo Chavez. Long in the crosshairs of U.S. military planners, Haiti's highly strategic Mole St. Nicolas landmass is situated on one side of the Windward Passage, directly facing Cuba. U.S. officials did not appreciate Aristide's recognition of Cuba hours before he left office in 1996.

U.S. intervention in the affairs of poor Latin American countries has a long and inglorious history. The most common reason for invasion in the past was unpaid debts. As the 20th century began, foreign powers, particularly Germany, France and the U.S., repeatedly sent gunboats into Haitian waters — usually to press the country to pay debts it simply could not afford. In one instance, U.S. marines secretly

entered Port-au-Prince and took the national treasure. A
desire to reclaim debt also precipitated the 1915 invasion,
culminating in twenty years of U.S. occupation and control
over Haiti's economy. While it would be a stretch to claim
the most recent overthrow of Haiti's government occurred
simply for the purpose of debt repayment, it is certainly
no coincidence that Haiti, like the other "failed states" of
Yugoslavia and Iraq, had massive "obligations" to foreign
bankers. "Failed state" may in fact be a euphemism for a
country's refusal to subject itself above all else to the claims
of international creditors.

Accruing debt of minimal benefit over which they
have no control has been standard fare for poor Haitians.
According to the Haiti Support Group, "About 40 percent of this debt [currently $1.2 billion] stems from loans
given to the brutal Duvalier dictators who invested pre-
cious little of it in the country." In fact Haiti became a
debt peon quite early in its history. Free Haitians in 1825
were forced to pay France 150 million francs ($22 billion
US in current purchasing power) as compensation to
French slaveholders for their loss of property. The slaves
had to reimburse the slave owners for their freedom.
The French also demanded preferential commercial
agreements and made sure French banks loaned Haiti
the money at high interest. Under the threat of invasion
(12 warships armed with 500 cannons were sent) and

exclusion from international commerce, the first payment of 30 million francs was made. In order to make this payment the government was forced to shut down every school in Haiti. Some have called this the very first structural adjustment program.

The need to repay France prompted President Boyer to implement the 1826 rural code, the foundation for "legal apartheid" between urban and rural people. In the countryside, movement was restricted, socializing after midnight banned, small-scale commerce limited, all in the name of increasing export crops to generate cash to pay France. The peasantry paid money to the state, receiving nothing in return. Late into the 19th century, payments to France consumed as much as 80 percent of Haiti's national budget. Only after 122 crippling years was the final payment on the debt made in 1947. (The debt was bought by the USA during the 1915-34 occupation and the final payments were made to that country.)

In the lead-up to Haiti's 200-year anniversary, Aristide initiated a campaign to pressure France to pay restitution for the $22 billion stolen from Haiti. This demand in itself provided France with sufficient motive for the removal of the Lavalas government. The installed regime that followed made no request for repayment. In fact, just after his inauguration, Latortue told Reuters that, "this [debt restitution] claim was illegal, ridiculous and was made only for political reasons ... This matter is closed. What we need now is increased cooperation with France." Strangely, on December 18, 2003, Latortue expressed a different opinion on the question of reparations in the Miami Herald, stressing "it's the moral and politically responsible thing to do." It was only when he was installed as de facto prime minister that he changed his tune.

The overthrow of Haiti's elected government is also intertwined with a deep-seated racism. Mainstream reporting on Haiti is run through with a sentiment that Haitians are helpless and destitute, unable to take care of their own affairs. That their destitution is directly attributable to 200 years of militarily enforced colonialism is never mentioned. That edifices in New York, Montréal and Paris were built on the backs of the Haitian poor is not recognized. That Haitians have, time and again, proven themselves to be anything but helpless, is apparently judged to be of little importance by mainstream journalists.

When abject poverty is the norm and one percent of the population owns 50 percent of a country, the election process is perceived as dangerous to the powerful. It is for this reason that the Haitian elite has never been comfortable with representative democracy; it is why they display considerable interest in subduing it. Aristide's removal was a clear message to the historically marginalized

— they can forget about changing their lot, they could forget about improving their lives. It was a crushing of the Haitian democratic spirit. This logic, however, will prove, as it has repeatedly over 200 years, to be flawed. If history is any indication, resistance will escalate to match the repression.

The final why of Canada's involvement with the coup and destabilization is that military and economic integration with the U.S. almost guarantees Canadian political support for that country's foreign policy, unless politicians feel substantial political pressure to act otherwise. Such pressure, especially in Québec, forced the Liberals from (officially) joining the Iraq debacle. This appeared to upset relations with the USA. Ottawa, therefore, needed to curry favor with Washington. It is not a coincidence that when the Liberals convened the "Ottawa Initiative" meetings in January 2003 they were also deciding to refuse political support for the Iraq invasion.

6 / How They Get Away With It
— Media Looks the Other Way

HOWEVER SYMPATHETIC TO U.S. foreign policy Canadian media may be, when contrasted to their counterparts in the USA, it is clear there is more honest coverage north of the border on issues such as the occupation of Iraq. An indicator of this difference is apparent upon entering the archives of Commondreams.org, a major U.S. leftwing website that regularly reprints international affairs editorials deemed critical of U.S. foreign policy from the Toronto Star — the most read newspaper in the country. So, have progressive-minded U.S. residents been getting their media coverage of Haiti from Canada as well? Quite the opposite. While activists have relied on sources like the Miami Herald and the Associated Press (sources not known to be critical of U.S. foreign policy) for basic information, the Canadian media has avoided mention of the police violence and political imprisonment that is a feature of daily life for the Haitian poor. Canadian media may be willing to criticize U.S. foreign policy, but if Haiti is any indication, they are much less interested in criticizing their own state's adventures abroad.

The grand distortion of events in Haiti by Canadian

media is an insidious routine that relies heavily on the downplaying and omission of information contrary to the Canadian government line — a line that would have us believe supporters of former President Aristide are largely to blame for Haiti's problems and that Canada's presence in Haiti has been benevolent.

Here is a small sample of what you didn't read in the Canadian news media:

On October 26, 2004, according to numerous eyewitnesses, Haitian police rounded up twelve young men in the Fort National slum. Police forced these men to the ground and shot them in the back of the head. Ambulances waiting nearby removed the bodies almost immediately. The affair was reported by numerous international media organizations and cited as an incident that required serious investigation by the United Nations special envoy to Haiti. Despite these dispatches, Canadian media barely reported on the killings. CBC online ran a single article and La Presse had a passing mention of the incident halfway through a 150-word blurb on Haiti. Aside from this, there was silence. Not one word of the incident in The Globe and Mail, National Post, Montréal Gazette, Ottawa Citizen, Toronto Star or Le Soleil. Two days after this incident, Haitian Police executed another four young men from Bel Air. This story was reported by a number of international media organizations yet stirred a resounding silence in the dominant Canadian media.

On October 13, 2004, Gérard Jean-Juste, a prominent Catholic priest and Lavalas supporter was arrested while serving food at his soup kitchen for impoverished children. It was revealed that three children were shot during the operation. A handful of Canadian newspapers reported on the arrest from the government's perspective and even then, not prominently. None of the seven papers mentioned earlier followed up on the story despite the release of statements condemning the arbitrary arrest by mainstream groups such as Amnesty International. Jean-Juste was arrested for disturbing the peace, a felony that Haitian law punishes with an 11 gourde — 40 cent — fine. Jean-Juste spent seven weeks in jail, eventually released as a result of international pressure. As this book went to press Jean-Juste was once again behind bars.

The March 2005 Harvard Law School report condemning the UN's mission to Haiti was almost entirely ignored by the Canadian media. The sole exceptions were a fine summary in La Presse and a short mention in Le Devoir. The even more disturbing University of Miami human rights investigation released at the end of January 2005 was also ignored. Exceptions to this were a passing mention in a Globe and Mail article, an opinion piece in the Toronto Star and the writings of a few progressive columnists.

At the end of April 2005, CARICOM once again confirmed its refusal to recognize Latortue. There was total Canadian media silence over the announcement. Little mention was made in Canadian media about CARICOM's refusal to recognize Haiti; to do so would be to bring into question the legitimacy of Canada's operations in Haiti. Any analysis of CARICOM's rationale for freezing Haiti's membership would unavoidably touch upon the question of legitimacy regarding the Latortue government. Canadians would begin to ask uncomfortable questions about their government's role in the removal of an elected head of state.

On June 4, 2005, Reuters reported that up to 25 people were killed in police raids on Bel Air over the weekend. On July 15 they reported on the UN massacre that happened the week before, as well as on two other HNP operations that left 22 dead. Neither story was picked up.

For news on Haiti, the Canadian media relies mainly upon wire services — Associated Press, Reuters and Agence France Presse — all three of which are sympathetic to the elite/western perspective. Still, as documented above, even when the wire services provide copy that contradicts the Canadian government position, Canada's media fail to pick it up. On the occasion that Canadian media do feel compelled to run copy that contradicts the official view, the stories are often either heavily truncated or modified. On March 1, 2005, Reuters reported that "Police began shooting as the demonstrators rounded a corner at an intersection, scattering the panicked crowd." The Associated Press reported that "As crowds passed the vehicle, police fired tear gas, then bullets. With weapons drawn, UN peacekeepers surrounded the area." CBC.ca, with no reporter on the ground, was compelled to offer this significant modification: "Police fired tear gas at the crowd *as they charged the roadblock*, then followed that with live ammunition" [emphasis added].

On the rare occasion when a Canadian reporter is sent to Haiti, the reports are marred with bias. A number of reporters were sent to Haiti during the armed rebellion and reported on Aristide's authoritarianism, drug connections and "thuggish" supporters, known as the Chimères. Canadian journalists gave little credence to other perspectives, preferring conversation with the French or English speakers that frequented the embassies and handful of elite hotels, rather than venturing into the Creole-speaking slums.

A January 15, 2005, article by the Globe and Mail's Marina Jimenez provides a clear example of post-coup journalism that does not stray far from the Canadian government line. In writing about Canada's ongoing role in Haiti, Jimenez did not look into the veracity of Paul Martin's claim — made two months earlier — that there were no political prisoners in Haiti. Nor did she discuss Canada's reasons for releasing aid, only two years after refusing aid to Haiti's democratic government based on claims of electoral irregularities in eight of 7,500 elected positions. Jimenez also completely avoided Canada's connection to an increasingly murderous HNP, which targets all, including children and journalists, who witness their misdeeds.

To her credit, Jimenez quoted a Haitian who said, "You, the Canadians, the French and the Americans ... sent Mr. Aristide into exile." Though Haitians widely believe as much, this is one of the few times the dominant media reported that Haitians believe Canada helped overthrow their elected government. Jimenez` article, however, mostly focused on the tough job facing a brave Québec City police officer who volunteered to help out in Haiti.

Reporting the truth in Haiti is a dangerous job. According to the Haitian Journalist's Association, many journalists in Haiti's northern and central regions have gone into hiding, fearing for their safety. On May 28, 2004, a cameraman for TeleTi Moun was arrested and spent several months in jail. Former rebels abducted and beat Lyonel Lazarre, a correspondent for Radio Solidarité and Agence Haïtienne de Presse, in the southern city of Jacmel after he reported on alleged police abuses. On May 15, 2004, Charles Prosper, a correspondent for Radio Tropic FM, was kidnapped and detained for two days by former rebels. Jeanty André Omilert was abducted in April 2004 and held for several days by anti-Aristide forces. In February 2005, gunmen shot Raoul Saint-Louis, co-host of a news show on Radio Megastar, not long after government officials criticized Megastar's reporting. A week after the coup, Ricardo Ortega, a correspondent for the Spanish television station Antena 3 was fatally shot. Initially "Lavalas bandits" were blamed, but subsequent investigation concluded that U.S. marines were the culprits. In March 2005, a reporter was killed while covering a UN firefight with ex-military. On June 4th, U.S. journalist Kevin Pina was beaten by an off-duty Haitian SWAT team officer. In January 2005, Abdias Jean, a reporter for a Miami-based radio station, was killed by the HNP after he witnessed officers execute three other people.

Joseph Guy Delva, head of the Haitian Journalists Association, Reuters correspondent and Aristide critic, has stated that if a journalist was arrested during Aristide's government, there would be a media uproar. Now, said Delva, when a journalist is arrested, "the newspapers and radio stations applaud." The reason for this change of heart is thinly veiled: The National Association of Haitian Media, a group of media owners that actively participated in the G-184, own approximately 20 of the 25 major media outlets in Haiti and uncritically disseminate anti-Lavalas propaganda.

Internationally, media groups aren't holding up their

end of the "watchdog" deal. The Reporters Without Borders (RWB) 2005 annual report claims that "Since the resignation of President Aristide, press freedom has increased ... The departure into exile of President Jean-Bertrand Aristide on 29 February 2004 ended a long nightmare for the Haitian media." Before the coup, RWB denounced the Aristide government but this group has barely mentioned the numerous attacks on the press since. RWB receives tens of thousands of Euros every year from the French government as well as funding from the National Endowment for Democracy and USAID. RWB also gets significant funding from a number of large corporations and has a contract with the Cuba Solidarity Center, a group closely aligned to Miami's right wing Cuban community and Roger Noriega.

7 / Resistance and What We Can Do

HAITI'S POOR DID NOT accept the kidnapping of their president. In the days following the coup property destruction and looting engulfed the capital — in a country where one percent of the population owns half of all property, its destruction is political. In a show of support for Aristide prior to the coup, hundreds of thousands marched on February 7, 2004, from Port-au-Prince up the hill to the wealthy area of Petionville. By all accounts, this march dwarfed any demonstration by the anti-Aristide opposition, even though there were credible reports that wealthy business owners coerced their employees into joining anti-Aristide marches.

Despite the lack of media attention in North America, opposition to the Haitian coup and occupation is mounting, led by countries and communities with large Black populations. CARICOM continues to refuse recognition of Latortue as prime minister. This position has been reaffirmed on numerous occasions despite significant U.S. pressure. The African Union, Cuba and Venezuela have adopted a similar stance. Those 69 countries continue to demand a UN investigation into the circumstances surrounding Aristide's removal.

The U.S. congressional Black Caucus denounced the 2004 coup and has made efforts to highlight the severe repression in its aftermath. Outspoken California Congresswoman Maxine Waters led a number of delegations to Haiti and regularly sends out press releases regarding human rights violations in the area. Even John Kerry, beholden to a black constituency, said: "They [the Bush administration] have a theological and an ideological hatred for Aristide. They always have. They approached this so the insurgents were empowered by this administration."

In June 2004, Argentine activists burned tires and threw firecrackers at the door of the Defence Ministry building after the country voted to send soldiers to Haiti. And in January of 2005, at the World Social Forum, a widely circulated resolution was passed condemning the coup. A month later Brazil's MST (landless workers movement) sent a delegation to Haiti and as a result the (supposedly) left wing Brazilian Workers Party government began to feel some pressure for that country's role in leading the UN military force. Pressure on Lula's government mounted on July 21, 2005, when protests were held at Brazilian embassies and consulates across North America in tandem with protests in Brazil against the July 6, 2005, UN massacre in Cité Soleil.

Ottawa and Montréal Haitian communities have led

resistance to Canada's crucial role in Haiti. Within weeks of the coup small Haitian support groups were formed across Canada. On March 10, 2004, in the House of Commons, the New Democratic Party's Svend Robinson called for the tabling of the Ottawa Initiative documents and for an investigation into Aristide's departure. That same day, NDP leader Jack Layton referred to the situation in Haiti as "very grave." But instead of "holding Paul Martin's feet to the fire" regarding Haiti, as the NDP claimed it would do at the time, the party dropped the issue. Not until a spate of mainstream press articles critical of the situation in Haiti were printed in mid-March of 2005, did the NDP finally release two press releases concerning human rights violations in Haiti.

Nearly one year after the coup, non-Haitian community consciousness took a significant step forward with the four-city visit of Haiti-based journalist Kevin Pina. Three weeks later there were actions across the country to commemorate the coup's one-year anniversary (and in as many as 50 cities worldwide). There was a 500-strong march in Montréal, the largest mobilization since the coup from within that city's Haitian community. In addition, over 100 demonstrators of non-Haitian descent attended the march — far more than the handful that attended the preceding Haitian solidarity protest. These actions generated both significant media attention and political energy. They were followed up by mobilizations in May and June against the Canadian government's international conference on Haiti.

Unfortunately the progressive Haitian community has not received much support in their struggle. Haiti still seems off the radar for most Canadians. Many are willing to march in the streets to criticize the U.S. over Iraq but have been unwilling to denounce our own government's substantial role in deposing the elected president of the hemisphere's poorest country. Knowledge about the situation in Haiti, particularly the significance of Canada's role, continues to be minimal.

But, the word is spreading. For example, StopWar.ca, one of Canada's largest anti-war coalitions located in Vancouver, has issued statements denouncing the coup and have organized educational events with local Haiti solidarity activists. It remains true, however, that there is a deeper reluctance to address the problem of Canadian "exceptionalism," which finds it much easier to criticize the U.S. than to turn that criticism towards our country.

It is clear that Canada has significant influence over the installed government. As well, Canada's government is far more likely to change its position on Haiti than its U.S. counterpart. It is also realistic to expect Brazilian activists to be able to influence their government in a direction less harmful to Haiti. If political repression directed against Haiti's social movements is eased, many Haitians have stated a belief in their own strength to overcome the country's small elite once again, allowing for the creation of a more just system. To accomplish this, the poor are first of all demanding a minimum level of respect and the return of their constitutional government, including the physical return of Aristide. Demanding the completion of a duly elected president's mandate is an important part of Haiti's refusal to accept arbitrary and outside intervention in their affairs.

There are numerous ways that Canadians can make a difference, from phoning MPs, to organizing meetings, demonstrating and occupying ministers' offices. Canadians can also arrange delegations to Haiti and help organizations that are taking great risks to document human rights abuses.

Ordinary people around the world owe a great debt to the people of Haiti. Two hundred years ago, Haitian slaves showed the world that freedom could be won and it is time for us to return the favor. We must offer real assistance, not "aid" that serves the interests of the rich and powerful. The least we can do is tell the truth about what governments have done in our name.

NOTE ON SOURCES AND REFERENCES

The Access to Information and Privacy office spokesperson first referred to over 1,000 pages pertaining to the original request for "all documents pertaining to the Ottawa Initiative on Haiti meeting." Only 63 pages were delivered and key passages were censored. These passages clearly pertain to comments made by then Minister of La Francophonie and Secretary of State for Latin America, Denis Paradis, and French Minister for La Francophonie Pierre-André Wiltzer. References to Aristide's eventual departure, return of the military, and the possibility of imposing a "Kosovo-model" trusteeship on Haiti (which have been reported elsewhere), are omitted. Several dozen other Access to Information and other requests have been or will be submitted, both in Canada, and United States. These are aimed at uncovering details of destabilization preceding the 2004 coup and the ongoing process of backing an illegal government.

HAITI WEBSITES

www.haitiaction.net – Haiti Action Committee
www.canadahaitiaction.ca/ – Canada Haiti Action Network
outofhaiti.ca — Canadian activist website
dominionpaper.ca – Grassroots National Newspaper
www.haiti-progres.com – Tri-lingual weekly newspaper.
ijdh.org – Institute for Justice and Democracy in Haiti
auto_sol.tao.ca – Haiti Resource Page
www.jafrikayiti.com – Haitian-Canadian activist Jean Saint-Vil
www.zmag.org – Znet "Haiti Watch" page
vwazanset.org – Haitian-Canadian anti-coup organization
teledyol.net/KP/HoH.html – Filmmaker Kevin Pina
www.margueritelaurent.com – Lawyer activist
ahphaiti.org/ – L'Agence Haitienne de Presse.
www.williambowles.info/haiti-news/index.html – Archive

REFERENCES

References by chapter and other resource aids are available on canadahaitaction.ca. Please also check for solidarity and other events.